George Riddle Wallace

Princeton Sketches

The Story of Nassau Hall

George Riddle Wallace

Princeton Sketches
The Story of Nassau Hall

ISBN/EAN: 9783337168711

Printed in Europe, USA, Canada, Australia, Japan

Cover: Foto ©ninafisch / pixelio.de

More available books at **www.hansebooks.com**

PRINCETON SKETCHES

THE STORY OF NASSAU HALL

BY

GEORGE R. WALLACE
CLASS OF '91

WITH INTRODUCTION BY

ANDREW F. WEST, PH.D.
GIGER PROFESSOR OF LATIN IN THE COLLEGE OF NEW JERSEY

ILLUSTRATED

G. P. PUTNAM'S SONS
NEW YORK   LONDON
27 WEST TWENTY-THIRD STREET   24 BEDFORD STREET, STRAND
The Knickerbocker Press
1893

COPYRIGHT, 1893
BY
GEORGE R. WALLACE.

Electrotyped, Printed and Bound by
The Knickerbocker Press, New York
G. P. Putnam's Sons

INTRODUCTION.

The traveller from the West or South, hurrying on his way to New York, is very apt to settle down to two hours of dreariness, as his train runs across the flat plain of New Jersey; yet, if he be an observant tourist, he will have occasion to notice, when half-way onward from Philadelphia, a distant view of the west. There, three miles away, on an elevated ridge, and backed by a range of blue hills, lies Princeton, embowered in its old elms, the many buildings of the university rising half buried in foliage, some of them silent witnesses of a glorious past, while more of them speak of the present and predict the more glorious future.

If he be a graduate, his eye will search the sky line until, in the middle of his view, he sees the slender belfry spire of Nassau Hall, the historic centre of the Princeton campus. Perhaps the monotony of the Jersey plain through which he has been riding makes the sight of this classic hill, graced with its green groves and sheltering shades, all the more charming; but, whether this be so or not, no Princeton man travelling that way ever fails, on passing Princeton Junction, to glance with fondness toward what seems to him, more and more as his years roll on, a true oasis of rest and happiness in his life's itinerary. If his train stops at the junction he will probably try the three-mile journey and revisit the old place. He will notice that the branch road, with its formidable grades and breakneck curves, once planned, as college tradition says, by a distinguished professor—well, he will notice that these are "iidem qui semper fuerunt," the same as they ever were—to use the classic words of that old Latin prose book now dead and gone, in which so many of our alumni were prepared for college. And as the puffing little engine toils up the last steep grade towards the Princeton station, though many a change will meet his eye which will gladden him as a lover of Princeton, and sadden him as he misses some cherished landmark, yet he will find many things still unaltered. If he be an alumnus of a generation back, there will be only a few professors of his old faculty to meet, and perhaps he is most likely to encounter first some old college servant with a half century's record, such as

Dennis, or Steve, or the indispensable and only James Johnson.

On glancing around he will notice at first only the wonderful change that has come over the place and, as with a wave of an enchanter's wand, transformed the quiet old college into the vigorous and active university. He will see the old college green enlarged into a park of hundreds of acres, stretching out over the hill and down the slope, with its twoscore beautiful buildings. He will learn of the growth of the faculty and will ascertain that it has increased in a ratio less only than the number of the students. He will be astonished at the multiplication of new departments, branches of study, elective and optional courses, the museums, observatories, laboratories libraries, apparatus, the various athletic grounds, and the many club-houses, and other organizations of the students. All these will seem new and strange to him, with the subtle fascination of the old and the ever striking charm of the new beauty. But if he stays a day or two, most of the lineaments of the old college as it was to him take shape again and revive, and the campus around Nassau Hall will still be found, as of old, the centre of all the university life.

Truly so and remarkably so in the beautiful October evenings, as the leaves are beginning to turn and the processions of students singing the college songs move to and fro; or better yet, in the still long evenings of May and June, just before the seniors leave and their singing sounds from the steps of Old North, when all the historic memories of the place, all the old student life at Princeton, back to the dim reminiscences of the Revolution and the colonial time seem to be evoked by the ever new magic of the old music. There under the trees planted in the time of Washington, the figures of the Revolution reappear to student imagination—Madison, Witherspoon, Ellsworth, Stockton, Freneau, Rush, "Light-horse Harry" Lee, the Bayards, Livingstons, Frelinghuysens, and all that company of noble souls who used their swords to achieve American freedom, or their pens to sign the Declaration of Independence and frame the Constitution of the United States.

But our prosaic muse is running away with us, and we are getting into the domain of Mr. Wallace's book. Suppose our traveller cannot stop at Princeton Junction. Suppose he is far away from Princeton. Then let him read this book, written newly by one who has lately passed out from under the Princeton elms. They too are the same as they ever were—but a little older, a little grander, a little more majestic. This book will take the reader in spirit to the old academic shades. There he may recline on the mellow sward and hear the seniors singing, and re-create in his own imagination that little world of university life, now lost to his sight, but living as truly as ever in his heart and life.

ANDREW F. WEST.

CONTENTS.

	PAGE
I.—IN GOOD OLD COLONY DAYS	1
II.—THE REVOLUTION	29
III.—THE HALLS	53
IV.—ANTE BELLUM	72
V.—ADMINISTRATION OF JAMES MCCOSH	101
VI.—PRINCETON UNIVERSITY	128
VII.—UNDER THE PRINCETON ELMS	149
VIII.—THE PRINCETON IDEA	179

Know all Men by these Presents, That I John Livingston of the City of New-York Merch*t* ~~~~~

For and in Consideration of of the Sum of Eighty Pounds ~~~~~~~~~~~ Current Money of the Province of New-York ~ to me in Hand paid at and before the Ensealing and Delivery of these Presents, by The Rev*d* M*r* Aaron Burr President of the College of New Jersey ~~~~~~~~~~~~ the Receipt whereof I do hereby acknowledge, and myself to be therewith fully satisfied, contented and paid: HAVE Granted, Bargained, Sold, Released, and by these Presents do fully, clearly and absolutely grant, bargain, sell and release unto the said M*r* Aaron Burr his heirs & assigns a certain Negro-Man named Caesar ~~~~~~~

To HAVE and to HOLD the said Negro Man Caesar ~~~~ unto the said M*r* Aaron Burr his ~~~ Executors, Administrators and Assigns for ever. And I the said John Livingston for my Self, my Heirs, Executors and Administrators, do covenant and agree to and with the above-named Aaron Burr his ~~~~~ Executors, Administrators and Assigns, to warrant and defend the Sale of the above-named Negro Man named Caesar against all Persons whatsoever. In Witness whereof I have hereunto set my Hand and Seal this Second ~~ Day of September Annoq; Dom. One Thousand Seven Hundred and Fifty Six. ⸺⸺

Sealed and Delivered in
the Presence of

D*s* Forman

John G Lansing

J*n*° Livingston

LIST OF ILLUSTRATIONS.

	PAGE
NASSAU HALL	*Frontispiece*
BILL OF SALE OF NEGRO	xii
PAPER EXECUTED IN 1748	xvi
PRESIDENT JONATHAN DICKINSON	3
FAC-SIMILE OF ADVERTISEMENT OF LOTTERY IN "THE PENNSYLVANIA JOURNAL," JANUARY 16, 1750	5
PRESIDENT AARON BURR	7
FAC-SIMILES OF LOTTERY TICKETS	9
MARQUAND CHAPEL AND MURRAY HALL	11
NASSAU STREET IN FRONT OF THE CAMPUS	15
BILL FOR REFRESHMENTS	19
THE OLD PRESIDENT'S HOUSE, NOW THE DEAN'S	23
SCHEME OF A LOTTERY FOR THE USE OF THE COLLEGE OF NEW JERSEY	26
THE BULLETIN ELM	27
PRESIDENT JONATHAN EDWARDS	30
PRINCETON UNIVERSITY	31
GRAVES OF THE PRESIDENTS	35
PRESIDENT JOHN WITHERSPOON	39
THE WEST CAMPUS, FROM UNIVERSITY PLACE	41

LIST OF ILLUSTRATIONS.

	PAGE
The Old Cannon.	45
Offices of Administration.	51
Clio Hall.	55
Alexander Hall.	63
Edwards Hall.	67
On the Campus—The Potter Woods	75
Prospect—the President's House	79
East College	83
Museum of Historic Art	93
West College	97
President McCosh	103
McCosh Walk	107
The School of Science	113
The Front Campus	117
On the Campus—View from Prospect	123
Bronze Statue of President McCosh in Marquand Chapel	131
The Dynamo House	135
The Magnetic Observatory	139
The Halsted Observatory	143
The Working Observatory	147
Under the Elms	151
Bonner-Marquand Gymnasium	155
The Brokaw Memorial Building and Swimming Tank	159
David Brown Hall	163
Albert Dodd Hall	169
Dickinson Hall	173

LIST OF ILLUSTRATIONS.

	PAGE
THE UNIVERSITY BOAT-HOUSE	177
WITHERSPOON HALL .	181
THE CHEMICAL LABORATORY	185
UNIVERSITY HALL .	189
REUNION HALL.	193
THE PRINCETON INN	197

This paper was probably executed in September, 1748, at which time Gov. Belcher succeeded in having Princeton fixed upon as a site for the College. *Vid.* Hageman's *History of Princeton*, vol. ii., page 243.

PRINCETON SKETCHES.

I.

IN GOOD OLD COLONY DAYS.

> Our weary travellers pass along,
> Cheered by the wildwood's merry song,
> To where old Princeton's classic fane,
> With cupola and copper vane,
> And learning's holy honors crowned,
> Looks from her high hill all around,
> O'er such a wondrous fairy scene,
> Of waving woods and meadows green,
> That, sooth to say, a man might swear
> Was never seen so wondrous fair.
> The Lay of the Scottish Fiddle.

In the ancient town of Newark, on the 9th of November, 1748, were celebrated the "Public Acts" of the first commencement of the College of New Jersey. Before the President's house six young men in black gowns, standing two and two, formed the head of a column. Behind them were the sixteen gentlemen named as

Trustees in the Royal Charter, while in the doorway stood the young President, Rev. Aaron Burr, in robe, bands, and wig, his gentle, intellectual face contrasting pleasantly with the shrewd and courtly expression of His Excellency Gov. Belcher, who, as President of the Board of Trustees, stood beside him, gorgeous in the court costume of the 18th century. At the order, "*Progredimini juvenes*," the procession moves to the church, the candidates walking uncovered. There is "an elegant oration in the Latin tongue" by the President, there are learned disputations in Latin by the candidates, an address by the *Orator Salutatorius*, delivered in "a modest and decent manner," not to mention other imposing ceremonies, before the degrees are conferred, "all which being performed to the great satisfaction of all present, His Excellency, with the Trustees and Scholars, returned to the house of the President in the order observed in the morning."

About two years before, on the 22d of October, 1746, the first charter of the college passed the Great Seal and was attested by John Hamilton, Esq., President of His Majesty's Council and Commander-in-Chief of the Province of New Jersey. Although the grants under this instrument do not seem to have been perfectly satisfactory, the Trustees proceeded at once to elect the Rev. Jonathan Dickinson President of the infant institution, and the first term began

PRESIDENT JONATHAN DICKINSON.

on the fourth week of May, 1747. We do not know how many students gathered at Elizabeth Town to enjoy the instructions of the President and his assistant, but the probability is that there were about twenty. For some years, Mr. Dickinson had been conducting an unchartered school for young men, which accounts for the fact that there was a class ready to receive degrees one year after the founding of the college. Like the more venerable universities of Europe, Princeton began with instructors instead of buildings, and the home of the President was the home of the institution.

President Dickinson was a man of remarkable energy and ability. Besides performing his duties as President, he was minister of a large parish and a practising physician of some repute. No man was more influential than he in founding the college, and the prestige of his great name as a preacher and controversialist, both in this country and abroad, gave it an assured position from the first. He broke down, however, under the strain of his excessive labors, and died before the end of the first academic year.

The Rev. Aaron Burr, a young man of thirty-one, but whose reputation was already made, was elected as his successor, and the college moved to his home at Newark. It was Mr. Burr's good fortune to begin his administration with the new charter, a much more liberal and satisfactory document, which had been procured through the interest of Governor Belcher.

Subscriptions are taken in by WILLIAM BRADFORD, at Sign of the Bible, in Second-Street

The Scheme of a LOTTERY, to be set up in Philadelphia.

For the Benefit of the New-Jersey College

To consist of 8000 Tickets at 30 s. each, 2152 of which to be fortunate, viz.

Number of Prizes	Value of each £		Total Value £
1	of 500	is	500
2	of 250	are	500
9	of 100	are	900
20	of 50	are	000
40	of 20	are	800
200	of 10	are	2000
1880	of 2 10 s.	are	4700
		First drawn,	40
Prizes, 2152		Last drawn,	60
Blanks, 5848			
			£. 10500
8000 Tickets at 30 s. each, is	l. 12000	From which deduct 12½ l. per Cent. is	1500

THE Drawing to begin on the 23d Day of April next, or sooner if sooner full, of which timely Notice will be given, that such Adventurers, as shall choose to be present, may see the Tickets put into the Boxes.

We hope those who wish well to the Education of the rising Generation, will encourage the Design ; which is to furnish the Youth with all useful Learning, and at the same Time to instil into their Minds the Principles of Morality and Piety.

The following Persons are appointed Managers of the Lottery, viz. *William Branson, George Spafford, Samuel Smith, Samuel Hazard, William Shippen, Joseph Redman, Andrew Read,* and *William Patterson* in *Pennsylvania,* and *James Hude, James Nelson;* and *Samuel Woodruff* in the *Jerseys* : Who are to give Bond, and be on Oath for the faithful performance of their Trust.

Prizes not Demanded within six Months after the Drawing to be deemed as generously given to the Use of the said College, and not to be Demanded afterwards, but applyed accordingly.

The Tickets will begin to be sold, by the Managers at their respective Dwellings, on the First Day of *January,* and also by *Peter Van Brugh Livingston,* and *William Peartree Smith,* in *New-York*

To be Sold, very cheap for ready Money, or short Credit, by

JOSEPH SIMS,

FAC-SIMILE OF ADVERTISEMENT OF LOTTERY IN "THE PENNSYLVANIA JOURNAL," JANUARY 16, 1750.

Little is known of the daily life of the college during the next eight years. The students lived dispersed in private lodgings, and attended the academic exercises, which were generally con-

PRESIDENT AARON BURR.

ducted in the county court-house. The county court-house was in those days the centre for the business, politics, and gossip of the neighborhood, and the demoralizing influence upon the students was felt to be so serious that only the "indefatigable industry and vigilance" of President Burr was able to guard against "the difficulties and dangers of these circumstances."

During the eight years' sojourn of the college in Newark, the Trustees were studiously engaged in devising means for the erection of suitable college buildings, particularly as they desired to remove the students at the earliest opportunity to a place "more sequestred from the various temptations attending a promiscuous converse with the world, that theatre of folly and dissipation." Newark is better now, but it was a sad town one hundred and fifty years ago. A number of prominent gentlemen in the colonies were appointed to canvass for subscriptions, lotteries were drawn, by permission of the provincial governments, in Connecticut and New Jersey, and two ambassadors were sent to great Britain to solicit funds. The Independents, Presbyterians, and Baptists of the mother country united with the clergy and laymen of the Established Church in raising funds, the Bishop of Durham being on record for a subscription of £5. Although the men most active in founding Princeton were Presbyterians, there were four Episcopalians and several Quakers on the first Board of Trustees, and the general response to appeals for funds at this time shows how thoroughly the college was recognized as a seat of learning without sectarian bias.

FAC-SIMILES OF LOTTERY TICKETS.

As early as 1750, the Trustees were able to make overtures to Prince Town and New Brunswick for a permanent location. The superior enterprise and public spirit of her citizens secured the prize for the former town, and on

September 27, 1752, the following entry was made in the minutes of the Board of Trustees:

"Voted, That the college be fixed at Princetown, upon condition that the inhabitants of said Place secure to the Trustees those two hundred acres of wood-land, and that Ten Acres of cleared land which Mr. Sergeant viewed; and also one thousand Pounds proc. money. The one half of which sum to be paid within two months after the foundation of the College is laid, and the other half within six months afterwards."

Nearly two years were consumed in completing arrangements, and it was not until July 29, 1754, that "Joseph Morrow first set a man to dig the college cellar."

For many years the college was the largest building in the colonies.

"This edifice being nearly finished, and considered as sacred to liberty and revolutionary principles, was denominated NASSAU HALL, from that great deliverer of *Britain* and assertor of protestant liberty, K. WILLIAM the IIId, prince of *Orange* and *Nassau*. It will accommodate 147 students, computing three to a chamber. These are 20 feet square, have two large closets, with a window in each for retirement. It has also an elegant hall of genteel workmanship, being a square of nearly 40 feet with a neatly finished front gallery. Here is a small, though exceeding good organ, which was obtained by a voluntary subscription. Opposite to which, and of the same height, is erected a stage for the use of the students in their public exhibitions. It is also ornamented, on one side, with a portrait of his late majesty, at full length;

MARQUAND CHAPEL AND MURRAY HALL.

and, on the other, with a like picture (and above it the family-arms neatly carved and gilt) of his excellency Governor Belcher. The library, which is on the second floor, is a spacious room, furnished at present with about 1,200 volumes, all of which have been the gifts of the patrons and friends of the institution, both in *Europe* and *America*. There is, on the lower story, a commodious dining hall, large enough to accommodate as many as the house will contain, together with a large kitchen, stewards' apartments, etc. The whole structure, which is of durable stone, having a neat cupola on its top, makes a handsome appearance; and is esteemed to be the most conveniently planned for the purpose of a college, of any in *North America*."

In the fall of 1756, President Burr moved with his flock of seventy students to the quaint old town on the King's Highway. A more favorable site could not have been chosen. Midway between the two great cities of the seaboard, "it stands on the first high land which separates the alluvial plain of South Jersey from the mountainous and hilly country of the north. There is a gentle depression between it and the mountain, and a gradual descent on either side of it, towards the streams that nearly encircle it." The town has spread itself comfortably over the broad tortoise-back hill, nearly encircling the campus, whose groves and towers occupy the highest part, and overlook the rich garden-lands of Jersey. Far to the south stretches an undulating champaign, whose varied expanse of field and forest is now dotted with farm-houses, or pierced by the ascending shaft of a white steeple, marking the site of some country village. Over thirty miles away, in the mellow haze of the horizon, the blue ridges of the Navesink Highlands trace the curving line of the coast. On the east, are the rolling foot-hills of the mountains, growing more rugged towards the north, while the western plain slopes gently to the Delaware River. Our founders are justified in regarding their new home as " not inferior in the salubrity of its air, to any village on the continent."

Unfortunately for this generation, no gossiping old traveller seems to have gone through New Jersey in 1756, and we do not know exactly how things looked to the new students. The chances are, however, that such a traveller would have seen a town very similar to that which met the eyes of the Marquis de Chastellux when he went through in 1780. The Marquis has left us an aged and time-stained volume of *Travels in North America*, in which he tells us that " beyond King's Town, the country begins to open and continues so to Prince Town. This town is situated on a sort of platform not much elevated, but which commands on all

NASSAU STREET IN FRONT OF THE CAMPUS.

sides; it has only one street, formed by the high road; there are about sixty or eighty houses, all tolerably well-built, but little attention is paid to them, for that is immediately attracted by an immense building, which is visible at a considerable distance. It is a college built by the State of Jersey some years before the war. It is situated towards the middle of the town, on a distinct spot of ground, and the entrance to it is by a large square court, surrounded by lofty palisades." This "square court" was that part of the campus in front of Old Nassau. As late as 1764 it was without a single tree, and the only harbinger of our glorious elms was a solitary bush in the yard before the President's house (now the Dean's). The two large sycamores standing before the Dean's house were planted by order of the Trustees in 1765, to commemorate the resistance to the Stamp Act.

In those days of classical models, college life was a little more stately than this irreverent age would be inclined to favor. It must have been a goodly sight to see the President, tutors, and students, all seated together in the wide dining-hall, clad in the scholastic gown, and arranged according to rank and seniority. They lived very substantially on "almost all the variety of fish and flesh the country here affords, and sometimes pyes."[1] At dinner they drank small beer or cider, and at supper, milk or chocolate. Young gentlemen who chose to indulge in that luxury were occasionally permitted to make "a dish of tea" in their apartments.

At five o'clock in the morning a large horn was blown in the entries, which, as a Freshman of the day sadly remarks, sounded like the last trumpet. This blast summoned the students to morning prayers. The students were not allowed to leave their rooms without permission, except for half an hour after morning prayers or recitation, an hour and a half after dinner, and from evening prayers until seven o'clock, on the penalty of four pence for each offence. Other college laws throw a curious light on the customs of the academic body in colonial days.

"None of the students shall play at cards, or dice, or any other unlawful game, upon the penalty of a fine not exceeding five shillings for the first offense; for the second, public admonition; for the third, expulsion. No jumping, hollaring, or boisterous noise shall be suffered in the college at any time, or walking in the gallery in the time of study. No member of college shall wear his hat in the college at any time, or appear in the dining

---

[1] To judge by the fac-simile of the bill of William Hicks, the annual Commencement dinners must have been somewhat more festive in character than has generally been supposed

The Trustees of New Jersey College Dr.

To Wm. Hick

1771 Sepr. 27th To 3 Dinners — £0..18..6
To 23 bottles of Wine a 5/- — 5..15..—
To 8 bottles Porter — 0..16..—
To 6 bottles of Beer — 0..9..—
To 3 Double bowls of Punch — 0..9..—
To 3 bowls Toddy — 0..6..—
To Tea for 13 Gentlemen — 0..13..—

£13..0..6

The above Acct Indors'd to Mr. Jno. Witherspoon

Princeton 12 Decr. 1771 Receiv'd of Mr. Sergeant
the above sum of Thirteen pounds Virginia
Proc. Money by me — William Hick

room at meal time, or in the hall at any public meeting, or knowingly in the presence of the superiority of the college, without an upper garment, and having shoes and stockings tight. Every scholar shall rise up and make obeisance when the President goes in or out of the hall, or enters the pulpit on days of religious worship. Every Freshman sent of an errand shall go and do it faithfully, and make quick return. Every scholar in college shall keep his hat off about ten rods to the President, and five to the Tutors."

The annals tell us that Oliver Ellsworth, of the class of 1766, was summoned before the college tribunal, charged with violating the last-named rule. Mr. Ellsworth made his defence after the following manner: "A hat is composed of two parts, the crown and the brim. Now this hat has no brim, consequently it is not a hat, and I can be guilty of no offense." The logicians of the Faculty found the syllogism correct, and the defendant was discharged, although it afterwards came out that the brim had been torn off with a view to making a test case. The student who displayed this legal sagacity was afterwards appointed Chief-Justice of the Supreme Court of the United States.

The old inns and taverns were no small feature of Princeton student life of the eighteenth century. Big, lumbering mail coaches, private carriages, heavy freight wagons, droves of cattle—the whole body of land communication between Philadelphia and New York rolled through the little town. Those wonderful coaches put on in 1766, which made the journey between the two cities in the unprecedented time of two days, and won for themselves the name of "flying-machines," dashed by the campus daily. All this travel enriched a number of inns whose names only remain. We hear of tavern signs such as "Hudibras," "Confederation," "Gen. Washington," "The College," "Red Lion," "City Hotel," "Mansion House," "Nassau Hotel," of which (excepting the last) the names only remain. We catch glimpses of students mingling with travellers in the wide inn-rooms, and indulging occasionally in heavy drinking and wild pranks, greatly to the scandal of "the superiority of the college."

It was at the "Nassau Hotel," kept by John Joline, "as arrant a tavern-keeper as any in Christendom," that Jas. K. Paulding, assisted by Washington Irving, composed that sparkling burlesque, published anonymously as *The Lay of the Scottish Fiddle*. In the third canto is a description of a *convivium*, which scarcely tallies with the rigid rules and solemn portraits that have come down to us from our academic ancestors.

THE OLD PRESIDENT'S HOUSE, NOW THE DEANS.

> "Around the table's verge was spread
> Full many a wine-bewildered head,
> Of student learned, from Nassau Hall,
> Who, broken from scholastic thrall,
> Had sat him down to drink outright
> Through all the livelong, merry night,
> And sing as loud as he could bawl,
> Such is the custom of Nassau Hall.
> No Latin now or heathen Greek
> The *Senior's* double tongue can speak,
> *Juniors*, from famed Pierian fount,
> Had drank so deep they scarce could count
> The candles on the reeling table."

while the "emulous Freshmen" were in a still worse condition. Such bouts, we may believe, were rare. But in the middle of the jollity, a travelling fiddler arrives,

> "And many lads and lasses, too,
> A buxom, witching, merry crew,
> As love's true gramayre ever knew,
> From country round have come, they say,
> To dance the livelong night away.
> Flew ope the door and in there came
> Full many a dancing, loving dame,
> With chintz short-gown and apron checked
> And head with long-eared lawn cap decked,
> And high-heeled shoes and buckles sheen,
> And bosom prank'd with boxwood green,
> With these, well paired, came many a lad
> With health and youthful spirits glad,
> To caper nimbly in Scotch reel,
> With toes turned in, and outward heel."

We will leave this goodly company to dance the night away. Some hours later the "students learned" will return to Nassau Hall, slipping quietly down the long corridors and turning their keys with a delicate consideration for the repose of the tutor next door. Next morning at five o'clock, in gown, with shoes and stockings tight, they will be in their accustomed chapel seats, looking like veritable incarnations of the rigid rules we read about. Some years later, in shabby continentals, they will be fighting the great battles of American independence, or, under the dignity of full-bottomed wigs, advocating in state and national halls the great measures of freedom. For among these students, whose fresh, youthful faces peep out from behind the classic masks, are those whose names will be held sacred by succeeding generations —men destined to guide armies, frame laws, sign with their own hand the Declaration, and one who will frame the document which makes us a nation and sit with honor in the presidential chair.

New-Jersey, December 12, 1763.

SCHEME
OF A
LOTTERY,
For the USE of
The College of *New-Jerſey*.

THE Legiſlature of the Colony of *New-Jerſey*, having been pleaſed to countenance this riſing Seat of Learning, ſo far as to paſs an Act, enabling the Truſtees to erect and draw a Lottery, for raiſing any Sum, not exceeding Three Thouſand Pounds Proclamation Money; it is hoped, that the generous Deſign in making this Law, will be carried into Execution, by all thoſe who wiſh well to the Inſtitution, or who are deſirous of promoting uſeful Knowledge in theſe infant Countries, and preparing our own Youth to ſuſtain the publick Offices in Church and State. The following Scheme is calculated for raiſing the Sum of Two Thouſand Nine Hundred and Ninety-nine Pounds Eighteen Shillings and Six Pence Proclamation Money: There are to be 13333 Tickets at Thirty Shillings each, whereof 4488 will be fortunate, ſubject to 15 per Cent. Deduction, *viz.*

Number of Prizes.		Value of each.		Total Value.
1	of	£. 1000	is	£. 1000
1	of	750	is	750
1	of	500	is	500
4	of	200	are	800
10	of	100	are	1000
20	of	50	are	1000
50	of	20	are	1000
100	of	10	are	1000
4299	of	3	are	12897
1	Firſt drawn	20	is	20
1	Laſt drawn	32-10	is	32-10

4488 Prizes.
8845 Blanks.

13333 Tickets, at Thirty Shillings each,   is   £. 19999-10

So that it is evident there are not Two Blanks to a Prize. The Drawing is to begin on the fourth Day of *April* next, at *Naſſau-Hall* in PRINCETON, or as ſoon before as the Lottery is filled; under the Inſpection of three of the Truſtees of the College. ROBERT OGDEN, and WILLIAM PEARTREE SMITH, Eſqrs, of *Elizabeth-Town*; JONATHAN SERGEANT, Eſq; of *Maidenhead*, and Mr. EZEKIEL FORMAN, Merchant, of *Princeton*, are appointed Managers, and will be under Oath for the faithful Execution of their Truſt.

TICKETS may be had of the ſeveral Managers; and of *Theunis Dey*, Eſq; in the County of *Bergen*; Dr. *Samuel Tuttle*, at *Morris-Town*; *John Ogden*, and *Nehemiah Baldwin*, Eſqrs, and Mr. *William Camp*, at *Newark*; Mr. *Joſeph Woodruff*, at *Elizabeth-Town*; *James Parker*, Eſq; at *Woodbridge*; *John Johnſton*, Eſq; at *Perth-Amboy*; *John Taylor*, Eſq; at *Middletown*; Mr. *James Robinſon*, at *Freehold*; *John Wetherill*, Eſq; near *Cranbury*; *James Hude*, Eſq; at *New-Brunſwick*; *Hendrick Fiſher*, Eſq; near *Bound-Brook*; *William Thomſon*, Eſq; and Mr. *Peter Schenck*, at *Milſtone*; *Richard Stockton*, Eſq; and Mr. *Jonathan Baldwin*, at *Princeton*; *George Reading*, Eſq; at *Amwell*; *John Hart*, Eſq; at *Hopewell*; *John Hackett*, Eſq; at the Union Iron-Works; *Samuel Tucker*, Eſq; at *Trenton*; the Hon. *John Ladd*, Eſq; at *Glouceſter*; *Edward Keaſbey*, Eſq; at *Salem*; *William Patterſon*, Eſq; at *Corytine-Bridge*; Mr. *David Stewart*, at *Reedy-Iſland*; *Elihu Hall*, Eſq; at *Octarara, Cecil County*; and Col. *Peter Bayard*, at *Bohemia*.

THE BULLETIN ELM.

II.

THE REVOLUTION.

> Nor shall these angry tumults here subside,
> Nor murders cease, through all these provinces,
> 'Till foreign crowns have vanished from our view
> And dazzle here no more,—no more presume
> To awe the spirit of fair Liberty ;
> Vengeance must cut the thread.
>   PHILIP FRENEAU, Class of 1771.

THE college had not been settled in its new home a year, when it was saddened by the death of President Burr. He had all of that charming personality and grace of manner which so distinguished his brilliant son. His tomb is in the Princeton graveyard, that "Westminster Abbey of America," as it has been called, and the moss-grown letters of the inscription bear eloquent testimony to the affectionate regard which he inspired :

> "O infandum sui Desiderium
> Gemit Ecclesia, plorat
>   Academia ;
> Ait Coelum plaudit, dum ille
>   Ingreditur
> In Gaudium Domini."

For the next decade a singular fatality seemed to hang over the presidential office. Jonathan Edwards was called from Massachusetts, and took charge of the college in January, 1758. He had just crowned his reputation as a pulpit orator and thinker by publishing his treatise on *The Freedom of the Will*, which gave him a place at once among the first philosophers of the world, and which still holds its position as the greatest metaphysical work America has produced. During the few months of his term his course with the

PRESIDENT JONATHAN EDWARDS.

Senior class produced so profound an impression "that they spoke of it with the greatest satisfaction and wonder." He had just begun his administration under the happiest auspices, when an unsuccessful inoculation brought on a disease from which he died on the 22d of March.

PRINCETON UNIVERSITY IN 1893.

He was in Princeton only long enough to leave her the heritage of his name.

In rapid succession the illustrious names of Samuel Davies and Samuel Finley[*] were writ-

[*] The following quaint letter from President Finley to the Rev. Eliezer Wheelock, who was the founder of Dartmouth College, is in the possession of the college:—

PRINCETON, Dec. 13, 1761.

REVD. & DR. BR.

I thank you for your Favour by Mr. Pomroy & your son, I am also under obligations for other like Favours, to which my constant Hurry, or want of Opportunity, prevented making any Return. Indeed, Hurry has been for years my constant plea ; & is so now.

Wou'd have wrote you a line in ye Fall, but heard you was to be this way in October, which prevented me. I examined your Son, & tho' he was less prepared than ye Rest of his Class, yet considering his age & good sense, I concluded he wou'd make a pretty good Figure in it, after some time, shou'd God grant him Health to Study; & so admitted him. And I can honestly say, yt his *being your Son* had no small influence on me ; & you may assure yourself, dear Sir, yt your recommendations at any Time, will *weigh heavy* wth. me.

I have not had opportunity to consult ye Commissioners for Indian Affairs ; but, if they are enabled to Support two at College I have not ye least Doubt of their Compliance with your Proposal. I speak dubiously because I have not yet got into ye State of affairs, & have none present of whom to enquire. I shall do all in my Power for your Son's welfare.

As to ye State of our College Mr. Pomroy can inform you. May ye Lord Jesus be with you, & prosper your Undertakings ! If God help me not I surely Sink.

I am

[SUPERSCRIPTION.]   Your affectionate Br.
    To The Revd.   & very hble. Servt.
  Mr. Eliezer Wheelock   Saml. Finley.
      at Lebannon
         In Connecticut.
By favr. of ye
  Revd. Mr. Benjamin Pomroy.

ten on the roll of our Presidents, until in 1768 Dr. John Witherspoon, the great War President, was called to the chair.

It scarcely needed the presence and example of so distinguished a Son of Liberty to arouse the enthusiasm of the student body in the great conflict which was rapidly coming to a crisis. Newsletters and the little weekly papers of the neighboring cities were eagerly read. Scarcely a day but some traveller climbed down from a dusty coach with new stories of oppressive measures in Boston or patriotic resolutions passed by the Burgesses of Virginia. The little band of patriots in Nassau Hall were true to the inspiration of that name. We catch glimpses of excited discussions around the great log fires of the inns, and fiery orations in the newly organized debating societies. Occasionally more positive demonstrations were indulged in.

In July, 1770, when the news came that the merchants of New York had broken through their resolutions not to import, there was great indignation at Princeton. A solemn procession was formed. The students, clad in black gowns, assembled in the centre of the college yard, and there, with fitting ceremonies, the bell tolling, they burned the letter which asked the merchants of Philadelphia to concur in the action of

GRAVES OF THE PRESIDENTS.

New York. All the students of this patriotic assembly, we are informed in a letter written by James Madison, were clad in American cloth. Among their number were a score of men who were to rise to distinguished positions in the State. That little group of about a hundred undergraduates sent four men to the Continental Congress, two to the Constitutional Convention, and eleven to the Federal Congress. It contained five distinguished Judges, four Governors of States, one Attorney-General, a Vice-President and a President of the United States.

During this period Philip Freneau had begun to write those *Poems of the Revolution*, which made his name a household word through the years of that struggle. On the commencement stage of 1771, he joined with Hugh Brackenridge in a poetic dialogue on "The Rising Glory of America." No less than sixteen of the poems published in his own edition of 1795, were written while in college. Freneau was a classmate and close friend of Madison, and, down to the time of his death in 1832, was accustomed to entertain his friends with stories of their college life, which, unfortunately, have not been preserved.

In January, 1774, there was another patriotic outbreak. It was the time when Governor

Hutchinson, of Massachusetts, was making his unenviable reputation, and fighting the battles of tea with Boston. A raid was made on the steward's quarters, and his entire winter's store of tea carried off to the campus. "We there burned near a dozen' pounds, tolled the bell, and made many spirited resolves." The effigy of Mr. Hutchinson, a canister about his neck, burned merrily with the tea.

It would require a large number of volumes to record the deeds of the Princeton men during the war. Two of her graduates and three of her officers signed the immortal Declaration, nine of the fifteen college graduates in the Constitutional Convention owed allegiance to Nassau Hall, and even a catalogue of her sons who brought honor to her name in field and forum would become tedious.

One staunch and rugged figure, however, stands out so prominently, and with so striking a personality, that he has identified himself inseparably with the history of his country and his college. Six feet tall and splendidly proportioned, he is said to have been second only to Washington in bearing and presence. His portrait in Nassau Hall shows a face with strongly marked features, a massive chin, a broad forehead, and an eye full of fire and decision. John Witherspoon joined in the first call for a Provincial Congress of New Jersey, and took an active part in preparing her republican constitution. In June, 1776, he was sent as a delegate to the Continental Congress, where he championed the then doubtful cause of inde-

PRESIDENT JOHN WITHERSPOON.

pendence. When a timid member suggested to him that the colonies were not yet ripe for that step, he answered, with characteristic Scotch vigor: "In my judgment, sir, we are not only ripe, but rotting."

When the Declaration was under debate, and the House was hesitating, Dr. Witherspoon arose, and, in the words of an eye-witness, "cast on the assembly a look of inexpressible interest and unconquerable determination, while on his visage the hue of age was lost in the flush of burning patriotism that fired his cheek." He closed his appeal with these words:

"For my own part, of property I have some, of reputation more. That reputation is staked, that property is pledged, on the issue of this contest; and although these gray hairs must soon descend into the sepulchre, I would infinitely rather that they descend thither by the hand of the executioner than desert at this crisis the sacred cause of my country."

An incident which occurred a few weeks after the Declaration was published, shows how President Witherspoon's services to liberty were recognized, both by friends and foes. The British troops of Staten Island arranged a little *auto da fé*. Effigies of the three Generals, Washington, Lee, and Putnam, were planted in a row, and before them the commanding figure of the venerable Doctor, who was represented as reading an address to his compatriots. The soldiers crowded around to enjoy the *rigor mortis* of the unfortunate gentlemen, and found great satisfaction in hurling imprecations at "the rebels," as they suffered the agonies of translation.

THE WEST CAMPUS, FROM UNIVERSITY PLACE.

The central position of Princeton, and the bold stand taken by the cluster of influential men residing here, drew upon the devoted village more than her share of attention from the enemy.

For three years after the opening of hostilities no commencements were held. The few students who remained to pursue their studies were voted their degrees at meetings of the Board of Trustees, held as opportunity offered. The President, with other officers of the college, was engrossed in public services, and a large number of students were fighting in the ranks. At one time the number of undergraduates was reduced to ten. New Jersey was a battle-ground, and as the tide of war swept back and forth along the old highway, Nassau Hall afforded barrack-room, first for one army, and then the other. There was never a time, however, when some members of the Faculty were not engaged in giving instruction to those who remained, and on each succeeding year a few degrees were conferred.

On the first of January, 1777, a brigade of Hessian troops arrived at Princeton, and were quartered in the church and college. The recitation rooms in the basement were used to stable the horses, and the benches carried upstairs for firewood.

Early on the morning of the third, the column set out to join Cornwallis at Trenton. The American army, shut in by the Delaware, was to be crushed that day, and the war ended. The whole world knows how Washington, leaving his camp-fires burning to deceive the enemy, swept around his flank, and fell upon the brigade at Princeton.

The first regiment of the Hessians had reached Stony Brook by the lower road, when they encountered in the gray dawn the troops of General Mercer, who had come to destroy the bridge, and hinder a pursuit by Cornwallis. A sharp contest, and the enemy were driven back through the town to the college. The main column of Washington's army found the rest of the brigade drawn up along the ridge just west of the present seminary grounds. Before an attack could be made they retreated to Nassau Hall, where doors were barricaded and windows broken out, in preparation for defence. Here, again, they made no serious stand, but on Washington's advance broke into open retreat. Some cannon shots fired by the Americans left marks on the walls, which can still be seen, and one ball, entering the chapel window, crashed through a full-length portrait of George II., removing his Majesty's head. Washington hur-

ried on to Morristown, where he went into winter quarters, but the sick and wounded were left at Princeton, and Nassau Hall was used as a hospital for six or eight months. In the desperate fighting at Stony Brook General Mercer fell, mortally wounded. The old Hale house is still standing on the battle-field, and the curious visitor can see the bullet marks on the woodwork, and the room in which General Mercer died. The battle left as a legacy two British cannon, both of which have had an eventful history, and one of which has become the great totem of the college.

When the enemy finally left New Jersey, the college was a complete wreck. Every accessible piece of wood, even to the flooring, had been used as firewood. All the ornaments, collections, and scientific apparatus were entirely destroyed. The library was burned or carried off, and years afterward some of its volumes were found in North Carolina, where they had been left by soldiers in Cornwallis' army. The Trustees at once took steps to repair the ruins, but the funds had fallen, and so late as 1782 only a few rooms in the basement and one or two above were fit to use. The rest of the building remained ruinous and tenantless. The Marquis de Chastellux, visiting Princeton about this time, found only forty students enrolled.

The commencement of 1783 was a notable event in the history of the college, and heralded the advent of a brighter era. Congress was then holding its sessions in the library room of Nassau Hall, and as a courtesy to their President, Elias Boudinot, who was a Trustee, and to the college which had placed its rooms at their disposal, the delegates, a number of whom were Princeton men, resolved to adjourn, and attend commencement in a body. An extended stage was erected in the church to accommodate the distinguished guests. On it were seated the Trustees and the graduating class, the whole of the Congress, the Ministers of France and Holland, and the Commander-in-Chief of the American Army. Ashbel Green, afterwards President of the college, was valedictorian. He closed his oration with an address to George Washington, which seems to have sustained Princeton's reputation for effective eloquence. The General, with characteristic modesty, blushed deeply, and, meeting the orator next day, congratulated him in such flattering terms that the valedictorian was put to the blush himself.

At this time General Washington begged the honor of presenting the college with fifty guineas. The Trustees accepted the gift, and voted to expend it in a portrait of the General, to be painted by Peale, of Philadelphia. The picture is full length, and represents the battle of Princeton in the background. It still hangs in the room where Congress met, adorning the frame which was occupied by George II., before that gentleman, in the excitement of the moment, lost his head at the battle of Princeton.

The closing years of Dr. Witherspoon's administration were devoted to those prosaic labors which repair the ravages of war. The minutes of the Board of Trustees are full of orders for restoring the buildings and schemes for filling the empty treasury. The venerable President retired to Tusculum, his countryplace, about a mile from the college, and found a partial relief from ceaseless activity in enjoying to some extent, to use his own phrase, a life of *otium cum dignitate*. With advancing age, his eyes paid the penalty for excessive labors, and the last days of the old patriot were passed in blindness, a trial which he endured with Miltonic heroism.

No place in America is more charged with memories of the Revolution than Princeton. The houses which the heroes of that struggle honored by their presence are still pointed out.

Every entering student must go over the battlefield and see just where the war for American independence was decided. The mossy stones of the ancient burying-ground bear names made familiar by the great struggle. The old cannons speak of the days when they knew the smell of powder, and Nassau Hall, second only in the wealth of its associations to Independence Hall, seems to look out from every antique window with a consciousness of its dignity and service in a former day. It is not strange that with such an atmosphere and such traditions, Princeton men have learned to consider the claims of their country, and have for a century and a half distinguished themselves in her service.

OFFICES OF ADMINISTRATION.

III.

THE HALLS.

The young patriots of Princeton found it impossible to live without a forum. The college had from the first given particular attention to training for public speaking. As early as 1750, a Freshman writes that they were required to "dispute once every week after the syllogistic manner," and shortly after we find the Seniors delivering monthly orations. The short administration of President Davies materially strengthened and confirmed this tendency. Himself a finished orator, and the most eloquent preacher of his day in America, he communicated to the students much of his own enthusiasm for the *ars artium*. It was at the commencement of 1760, a year after President Davies' inauguration, that "Mr. Benjamin Rush arose, and in a very sprightly and entertaining Manner delivered an ingenious Harangue in Praise of Oratory. Then followed a Forensick Dispute in English, in which it was held that 'The

Elegance of an Oration much consists in the words being Consonant to the Sense.'" "The elegant, pathetic valedictory oration," which concluded the exercises, adds its testimony to the fact that the art of speaking was at that time very generally and successfully cultivated.

It was among such a body of orators, fired by the burning questions of the time, that Princeton's venerable halls had their birth. These organizations were first known as the Plain Dealing and the Well Meaning Societies. Unfortunately, the records of the early societies have perished, and the exact dates and circumstances of their origin cannot be positively determined. Dr. Giger, in his *History of the Cliosophic Society*, proves conclusively that the Well Meaning Society was in existence in 1765, and presents evidence of its foundation in that year by William Patterson and others. Dr. Cameron, the historian of the American Whig Society, says of the Plain Dealing Club: "We are satisfied that it was in existence in 1763 and was founded at an earlier date, probably in 1760." Whatever the birthdays of these clubs may have been, there is no doubt that for some years they flourished side by side, and devoted themselves mainly to the discussion of political questions. The rivalry soon became so intense,

however, that their discussions assumed a decidedly local character. The battles of Frederick the Great, and the right of Parliament to tax the colonies, were alike forgotten in a "paper war," of which only the distant echoes have reached us. Fierce satires and innumerable lampoons were exchanged by the combatants, to the great edification of the college at large. We cannot find just what the *casus belli* was, and indeed one of the spectators of the strife, writing under the name of "Censor," assures us that after conversing with persons in as well as out of the societies, he was utterly unable to learn the cause of all this "clatter of violence."

The Faculty finally decided that the only way to restore peace was to kill the societies, and consequently an edict was issued some time in the year 1768, closing their doors. The only relic of their existence which has survived the lapse of time is a quaint old diploma, issued by the Plain Dealing Club in 1766.

"OMNIBUS ET SINGULIS

"Has literas lecturis, notum sit. quod JOSEPHUS HASBROUCK, A. B., perdigne se gessit dum inter nos versatus fuit, et præterea quamdiu se ita gesserit, omnia ejusdem privilegia jure sibi vindicet. Cujus sigillum commune

Plain Dealing Club, nominaque nostra subscripta Testimonium sint."

[seal.] [signatures.]

"Datum Plain Dealing Hall in Aula Nassovica quarto calendas Octobris, Anno Aerae Christi millesimo septingentesimo et sexagesimo sexto."

For about a year there were no societies, but after the smoke of the battle had cleared away and the passion of the "paper war" was in a measure forgotten, they were permitted to revive again under different names. On June 24, 1769, James Madison, with some of the members of the Plain Dealing Club and some other students, formed the American Whig Society. On the eighth of June, 1770, seventeen under-graduates met and reorganized the Well Meaning Club under the name of the Cliosophic Society.

For fifty years, these dates of 1769 and 1770, respectively, appeared on the diplomas and medals of the reorganized societies as the years of institution. In 1820, however, the Cliosophic Society decided to assume the date of the foundation of the parent club, and since that time has written *Funditur 1765*. The Whigs have never seen fit to follow this example, partly because it is impossible to determine the exact year in which the Plain Dealing Club was founded, and partly because they are content to point to the reorganizers of 1769 as their charter members. Both societies are fortunate in the illustrious coterie of men whose names head their rolls.

The rechristened societies were received into the favor of the Faculty, and assigned rooms on the fourth (now the third) floor of the college. Shortly after, the " paper war " broke out again, though in a milder form. Lampoons were read before the college in the Prayer Hall, or posted up on the doors. Some idea of these productions may be formed from the following specimen, written by Philip Freneau, the poet of the Revolution, in honor of an unfortunate member of the Cliosophic Society.

THE DISTREST ORATOR.

" Occasioned by R. A――――'s memory failing him in the midst of a public discourse he had got by rote."

> Six weeks and more he taxed his brain,
> And wrote petitions to the Muses—
> Poor *Archibald!* 't was all in vain,
> For what they lent your memory loses.
> Now hear the culprit's self confess
> In strain of woe, his sad distress :

"I went upon the public stage,
I flounced and floundered in a rage,
   I gabbled like a goose ;
I talked of *custom, fame* and *fashion,*
Of *moral evil* and *compassion ;*
    And pray what more ?

"My words were few, I must confess,
And very silly my address—
   A melancholy tale !
In short, I knew not what to say,
I squinted this and the other way,
   Like Lucifer.

"'Alack-a-day ! my friends,' quoth I,
'I guess you 'll get no more from me—
   In troth I have forgot it !'
O ! my oration ! thou art fled,
And not a trace within my head
   Remains to me.

"What could be done ? I gaped once more,
And set the audience in a roar ;
   They laughed me out of face.
I turned my eyes from north to south,
I clapped my fingers in my mouth,
   And down I came !"

Many a modern Clio and Whig who reads these lines will smile as he recalls his own maiden efforts, and reflect that times have not changed so much after all.

These mimic battles were soon obscured under the shadow of a more portentous war-cloud. On the 29th of November, 1776, tidings reached the college of the approach of the enemy.

" Our worthy President, deeply affected by the solemn scene, entered the hall where the students were collected, and, in a very affecting manner, informed us of the improbability of continuing there longer in peace ; and after giving us several suitable instructions and much good advice, very affectionately bade us farewell Solemnity and distress appeared in almost every countenance. Several students that had come five or six hundred miles, and just got settled in college, were now obliged, under every disadvantage, to return with their effects, or leave them behind, which several, through the impossibility of getting a carriage at so confused a time, were obliged to do, and lost their all."

In the general confusion, the halls did not escape. Although something in the way of college instruction was *en évidence* throughout the war, and degrees were given to a few students every year, the halls were entirely discontinued, and when peace was finally restored, the few hall men who remained in connection with the college returned to find those sacred chambers which had guarded their mysteries in sad and utter ruin.

Clio was the first to revive. Her old room was repaired, and on July 4, 1781, the first meeting was held and the work of the society resumed. The Revolution almost destroyed the Whig Society. There were but two Whigs in the class of 1781, and in 1782 but one member of the hall in college. In the spring of that year, however, the society was revived, and met in the college library until their room was repaired.

On the 4th of July, 1783, at the celebration of the national jubilee, the halls for the first time elected an orator to represent them before a public audience. The orators of the day spoke before Congress, which was then sitting at Princeton, and afterwards dined with its President, and other invited guests, at Morven, the old Stockton homestead. From this time down until 1840, the halls united in selecting a man to read the Declaration of Independence on each returning Liberty Day. The custom of appointing four orators from each hall to represent it on the evening before commencement, originated some time between 1783 and 1792. Until 1865, these orators were elected by vote of their respective halls. Old graduates tell of the notable canvasses and elaborate intrigues by which oratorical aspirants sought to gain the coveted

ALEXANDER HALL.

honor. To remedy the evils growing out of this method, in 1864 it was decided to choose the orators in a contest before judges elected from the graduate members of hall. This plan continues to give complete satisfaction. Shortly after this change, a further stimulus was given by offering four medals to be contested for by the speakers, and the Maclean Prize of $100 to be awarded for the best written oration. In 1876 Mr. Charles R. Lynde presented to the college the sum of $5,000, the interest of which is divided into three prizes, to be competed for annually by three senior debaters chosen from each hall. There are, of course, a number of other prizes offered by the college for excellence in writing, speaking, poetry, and debate; but although hall emulation extends to the contests for them, the prizes themselves are offered to the college at large. Each hall has also an elaborate "prize system," by which it seeks to stimulate its own members to their best work.

The fire of 1802 brought another heavy disaster upon the societies. Their rooms were just under the belfry where the conflagration broke out, and their property, including many valuable records, was almost completely destroyed. Old Nassau Hall seems to be rather indifferent to fire, though, and it was only a short time before the gutted rooms were repaired, and furnished with an increased splendor. We have an account of the appearance of Clio in 1805, as it came from the hands of the renovators.

"There were four raised platforms, one on each side. On the north side were the chairs and desks of the principal officers, upholstered with red damask. Settees were placed against the walls, and chairs formed the other seats. The floor was covered with an expensive carpet. The window curtains were of white dimity and red damask. A chandelier was suspended by iron chains from the centre of the curved ceiling, and lustres hung around the walls, with glass lamps in the sockets. The walls were covered with velvet paper of a beautiful pattern. The room in summer was unpleasantly hot, the ventilation being very imperfect, and when the membership increased it became almost intolerable. . . . To crown all, the roof leaked badly."

The quarters of Whig, across the hall, doubtless shared with those of Clio both the elegance and the discomforts of this description.

1838 is writ large in the histories of the halls. In that year they moved into those beautiful Greek temples which live in the memories of the alumni of more than fifty years. They were in the Ionic style. The columns of the hexastyle porticos are copied from those of a temple on the Ilissus, near the fountain of Callirhoe in Athens. The temple of Dionysus,

EDWARDS HALL.

in the Ionian city of Teos, furnished a model for the buildings in other respects. Elegantly furnished and equipped with good libraries, these halls formed in many respects the centre of college life. In them, generations of men have passed through the metamorphosis from stammering and blushing freshmen to suave and eloquent seniors, and then gone forth to honor their halls in the pulpit and at the bar. Thousands of alumni cherish in the tenderest corner of their hearts, memories of long hours spent in the recesses of the old libraries, of life-long friendships formed within those mysterious doors, and of exciting crises on the floors, when the gray-haired ministers and learned judges of to-day were compassing heaven and earth to carry a motion of adjournment or bending all their energies to entangle their President in the meshes of parliamentary law.

The old halls have gone. They had become inadequate to the growing needs of the college, and in 1889 the work of demolition was begun. In their places, stand two splendid temples of white marble. The pure Greek of the old buildings has been retained, and the double façade on the southern side of the quadrangle looks like a glimpse of the Acropolis. Within these buildings are commodious libraries, reading-rooms, club rooms, and in each a spacious senate-chamber, where proper resolutions concerning the great questions of literature and politics will continue to be argued and adopted.

In their origin, the halls of Princeton have much in common with similar organizations formed in the provincial colleges. Harvard, Yale, William and Mary, and Columbia, all had literary clubs formed on practically the same basis. The unique thing about the Princeton halls is that they seem to have absorbed the good old Calvinistic doctrine of "final perseverance." Of the many societies which were contemporaries of Clio and Whig in their younger days, not one remains. They have either disappeared altogether, or have been absorbed in the Greek-letter fraternity movement and entirely lost their original character. Both of the Princeton halls have had repeated requests to establish chapter houses in other colleges, but they have uniformly refused to join the fraternity movement.

The result has been most happy for Princeton. Instead of a number of small competing fraternities, she has two noble and venerable institutions, large enough to engage in heroic competitions for literary honors and dignified enough to stay out of petty rivalries in college affairs which do not directly affect their interests.

At each returning commencement, the fathers gather to revive old memories, and hear what the undergraduates have been doing in the preceding year. The mysteries which are concealed behind those marble columns and massive doors are too awful to be divulged, but it is said that inquisitive persons who linger near the portals, occasionally hear rumblings of thunder like unto the ten-pin games of Heinrich Hudson, and the muffled sounds of voices and applauding hands. It is inferred from these phenomena that there is within the halls some magic influence which warms the blood and renews the youth of the gray-haired fathers, and that the younger members, catching the spirit of their sires, come forth with renewed enthusiasm for their halls, a veneration for their past, and an increased confidence in their future.

IV.

ANTE BELLUM.

During the last few years of Dr. Witherspoon's presidency, the burden of administration had been carried by the Vice-President, Samuel Stanhope Smith; and on the death of the old War President in 1794, there was no question as to who should be his successor.

The history of Princeton can be rudely divided into three epochs. The first, extending from its foundation in 1746 to the close of the century, was marked by a remarkable cluster of brilliant men who were identified with the college either as officers or patrons. In the stirring events of that heroic age, these men rose to an eminence which gave their college a singular prestige throughout all the colonies, and even beyond the sea. Her reputation received added lustre from the young alumni, an unusually large proportion of whom became men of distinction and wide influence. George Washington, writing to his adopted son, a student in Princeton at the time, after referring to some change in the course of study which had been recommended by one of the tutors. says:

"Mr. Lewis was educated at Yale college, and, as is natural, may be prejudiced in favor of the mode pursued at that seminary; but no college has turned out better scholars or more estimable characters than Nassau. Nor is there any one whose president is thought more capable to direct a proper system of education than Dr. Smith."

Similar expressions in the letters of other eminent men show how closely Princeton, as an institution, was identified with the life of the time.

With the dawning of the nineteenth century began an epoch of less dramatic if not less substantial influence. The long list of senators, governors, cabinet officers, judges, and other prominent men in Dr. Maclean's history, who held diplomas from Princeton, shows that her influence had not abated. At the same time they were not so distinctively known as Princeton men, and the college itself did not stand out so prominently before the country.

It must be confessed, too, that at the beginning of the century an unfortunate policy in the discipline of the college had the effect of increasing the disorders it was intended to suppress. A spirit of opposition to authority became prevalent, which developed at times into open warfare. Organized rebellion and wild pranks were punished with a Draconian rigor, displaying more sternness than tact; and the natural result was, not only to lessen the enthusiasm of alumni, but also to perpetuate a tendency to outbreaks, the reports of which injured the reputation of the college. The responsibility for this injudicious course seems to have rested in some degree with the Trustees. They interfered to an unprecedented extent with the details of administration, and were naturally less competent to deal with difficult questions than the President and Faculty, who were on the ground, and were thoroughly acquainted with all the aspects of every case which arose.

The temptation to such outbreaks was greater then than it is now. There was very little athletic work of any kind, and efforts in that direction were regarded with scant favor by a Faculty which had not learned the value of these exercises in teaching self-control and encouraging a manly spirit. As a result, the irrepressible vitality of healthy young men found outlet in many a cunningly devised and daringly executed plot. A quaint entry upon

ON THE CAMPUS. THE POTTER WOODS.

the minutes of the Faculty, in the closing years of Dr. Witherspoon's administration, shows the attitude of that body toward athletics, and records the first appearance of base-ball at Princeton.

"Faculty met Nov. 26, 1787.—It appearing that a play at present much practiced by the small boys among the students and by the grammar scholars with balls and sticks, in the back campus of the college, is in itself low and unbecoming gentlemen and students; and inasmuch as it is attended with great danger to the health by sudden and alternate heats and colds; as it tends by accidents almost unavoidable in that play to disfiguring and maiming those who are engaged in it, for whose health and safety as well as improvement in study as far as depends on our exertion, we are accountable to their parents and liable to be severely blamed by them; and inasmuch as there are many amusements both more honorable and more useful in which they are indulged,—Therefore the Faculty think it incumbent on them to prohibit the students and grammar scholars from using the play aforesaid."

College government, too, was a much more difficult thing then. It is hard for the undergraduate of to-day, when the tone of the college is so distinctively Christian, to realize the moral atmosphere of seventy-five years ago. French philosophy was still fashionable, and French skepticism was carefully cherished by young men as the badge of polite learning and freedom. The gay and reckless spirit which always accompanied this philosophy of life was not wanting. It was necessary to ride hard, drink deep, and fear nothing. At one time there were only twelve students who acknowledged their adherence to the old faith, and even so late as 1841, when the venerable Dr. Theodore Cuyler was an undergraduate, the little band of Christians were dubbed the *religiosi*, and met in a little room in the top of Old North.

When we remember, too, that good preparatory schools were rare then, and the men in college were, as a rule, much older than they are now, it will not seem strange that the enforcement of proper regulations was no easy task.

After the '20's, the spirit of disorder gradually subsided, and during the peaceful reigns of Presidents Carnahan and Maclean, the college gathered strength for the brilliant university era which was heralded by the inauguration of Dr. McCosh, in 1868.

Washington Irving's published works give us a glimpse of the student life under Dr. Smith, as it appeared to the genial writer for *Salmagundi*. Under date of February 24, 1807, appears "Memorandums for a Tour to be Entitled

PROSPECT—THE PRESIDENT'S HOUSE.

'The Stranger in New Jersey; or, Cockney Travelling.'" Chapter IV is outlined as follows:

" Princeton—college—professors wear boots !—students famous for their love of a jest—set the college on fire and burned out the professors ; an excellent joke, but not worth repeating—Mem. American students very much addicted to burning down colleges—reminds me of a good story, nothing at all to the purpose—two societies in the college—good notion—encourages emulation, and makes little boys fight ;—students famous for their eating and erudition—saw two at the tavern, who had just got their allowance of spending money—laid it all out in a supper, got fuddled, and d——d the professors for nincoms, N. B. Southern gentlemen . . . commencement—students give a ball and supper—company from New York, Philadelphia and Albany—great contest which spoke the best English . . . students can't dance—always set off with the wrong foot foremost . . ."

Washington Irving never had any experience with the disciplinary side of college life, but he seems to have made up for it by a close and conscientious study of its convivial aspects, and he and his jovial *confrères* were well-known and welcome guests at the ancient Princeton inns.

The most memorable event in the annals of President Smith's administration was the destruction of Nassau Hall by fire, on the 6th of March, 1802. The building was completely gutted, the library and most of the philosophical apparatus destroyed, and nothing was left of the college save the bare, brown walls. These old walls, built of a ferrous sandstone, have survived the sack of the edifice by the British, and two subsequent conflagrations. Erected with provincial honesty, and of a material alike indifferent to fire and weather, they are as staunch and clean to-day as when the rural Jerseyman came, with open-mouthed wonder, to the dedication of the largest building in America.

A thorough investigation was made, but without finding any proof of incendiarism. The Trustees issued an address to the "inhabitants of the United States," asking for aid; the President returned from a western and southern tour with $40,000, and in a short time the college was rebuilt in a substantial manner.

At the commencement of 1806, fifty-four men were graduated, the largest class down to that time. There were about two hundred men in college; the number of students was constantly increasing, and the outlook was very gratifying, when suddenly the " Great Rebellion " of 1807 broke out, in which the rebels were worsted, with loss of half their number. For some reasons not certainly known, a spirit of discontent had been growing, which finally culminated in open revolt.

EAST COLLEGE.

The conspirators made their arrangements with the boldness and skill of many Catilines. Old North was stocked with provisions for a long siege, troops were thoroughly organized, and on a prearranged signal every door was barricaded, and all the lower windows blocked with firewood. History leaves us to imagine the onslaught of the President and his trusty cohort of instructors, the threats of dire punishment, and the stern defiance hurled from the deep embrasures of third-story windows. Within the beleaguered walls, the ancient order of the Roman Republic was revived with a fidelity which reflects the highest credit on the classical instruction of the college. Two consuls held sway over an elaborately organized state. It is not known whether internal feuds, famine, or overwhelming assaults from without led to capitulation, but certain it is, that after several heroic days the tutors were again in possession of the entries, and the *fortes viri* of the republic were reduced to the ignominious position of disorderly students.

A guard of citizens was called in to protect college property, and an investigation instituted which resulted in the dismissal of a number of offenders and the censure of others. The men were not satisfied, however, and presented a petition which was regarded by the Faculty as offensive. The students were assembled, and informed that the roll would be called; that every student might answer to his name and either separate himself from the combination or adhere to it.

"When this business was about to be begun, one of the leaders of the association rose and gave a signal to the rest, and they rushed out of the hall with shouting and yelling. . . . The Faculty declared to the students that those who were going in this riotous manner were now suspended from the College."

Out of two hundred students, one hundred and twenty-five were suspended, nearly half of whom afterwards returned. Thus ended the Great Rebellion,—a fantastic episode, but one which left a deep mark on the college. It was many years before the catalogue again showed an enrolment equal to that which preceded the siege of Old North.

On the retirement of President Smith in 1812, Dr. Ashbel Green, the valedictorian who had enjoyed the honor of addressing Washington and the Continental Congress in 1783, was unanimously elected by the board to succeed him. Dr. Green entered upon the duties of his office with a nervousness and trepidation which may have contributed a little to the realization of the difficulties he feared. "My first address to the students," he says, "produced a considerable impression, insomuch that some of them shed tears. This greatly encouraged me ; but the appearance was delusive or fugitive. Notwithstanding all the arrangements I had made, and all the pains I had taken to convince them that their own good and the best interests of the institution were my only aim, I had the mortification to find that the majority of them seemed bent on mischief." One cannot escape the conviction that the good Doctor exaggerated the situation a little, for only a year or two before, a committee of visitors had reported " that during the present session the students of the college have been in general attentive to their studies, and that great order and regularity have been observed in the dining room." [1]

[1] The following letters from President Green are interesting as showing his views upon the state of affairs.

PRINCETON, April 12, 1815.

REVD. & DEAR SIR:

I yesterday received three copies of your sermon entitled the "Gospel Harvest," for which I sincerely thank you. On the envelope to request an account of the "glorious revival" of religion in the college here. It has been truly glorious. We number between 40 & 50 hopeful converts, in the last four or five months. But the trustees of the college, at their last meeting, have directed me to publish the statement which I made to them on this interesting subject. I am now preparing it for the press, & expect it will be

Although from the first "every kind of insubordination that they could devise was practiced," published in a few days. A copy shall be immediately forwarded to you.

This morning I have had the great gratification to learn, by a letter from Mr. Gallaudet of Hartford, that a remarkable revival of religion has begun in Yale college. By his representation it appears that there is a wonderful similarity between what is taking place at Yale, & what was witnessed here in January last. Labourers in the gospel vineyard, & reapers of the gospel harvest, will, I trust, be provided by these dispensations of divine grace & mercy. If any thing short of the power of God could convince infidels of the excellence of evangelical principles, I should suppose it would be a view of the change which is made on the tempers & in the lives of those, On whose hearts these principles have made a practical impression. Never, certainly, have I seen youth so amiable, & in all respects so promising, as the mass of those who now compose the students of Nassau Hall. A year ago this was far, very far, from being the fact. The change has manifestly been wrought by the finger of God, & to him be all the praise.

I wait with a degree of impatience for the communication which you have promised to make.

With best regards to Mrs. Morse, I am, affectionately & sincerely
                                        Your friend & brother
Dr. Morse.   A. Green.

                                        Princeton, June 14, 1817.
Revd. & dear Sir :

You are not ignorant that the present Vice President & professor of Mathematics & Philosophy expects to vacate his place in the college here, at the end of the present session. It will be highly injurious to the interests of the institution, if the important professorship in question be either left open, or badly filled. Yet to find a person calculated, in all respects, to fill it advantageously, may be a matter of no small difficulty. Such a person I do not know. I know a number who have science enough. But not one whom, on the whole, I could recommend. The design of this letter is to request you to look round you & make inquiries, in your region of country & acquaint-

the first flagrant outbreak occurred on the 9th of January, 1814, when " a little after nine

ance, for a suitable man to take the place of professor Slack. As to the Vice Presidency I think it most probable that it will be attached to Mr. Lindsly, if he will consent to take it. It is much to be regretted that this office was ever instituted. It is utterly useless ; & it has proved a millstone about the neck of the present occupant, which has had more influence to sink him than every thing beside. The contemplated professor ought to be a man of religion, & of accommodating temper & manners ; & a young man will do better than an old one.

Nothing can exceed the peace & order of the college from the commencement of the session till the present time. We have not had a case of discipline. But this was the fact also last winter, till within ten days of the riots. I hope the present calm is not the precursor of another storm. That storm, however, has not hurt but helped us. I believe there never was such an accession of students to the college, in the Spring of the year, since it existed, as there has been this Spring. The house is full, & there are 8 with Mr. Lindsly, waiting to enter. Such is the issue of the gloomy prognostications of some, who probably wished what they foretold, & are vexed that their predictions have proved to be false. I have always believed & said that the publick would bear us out in a strict question of discipline ; & that the college would not sink but rise under it. The late occurrence has verified this opinion, even beyond my own calculations. A former rebellion was the consequence, undoubtedly, of a total relaxation of government ; & the institution instantly sunk & never rose again under the administration in which it occurred. With these unquestionable facts staring them in the face, it does seem a little strange that certain men speak & act as they do. For two or three weeks past there has been an increasing seriousness in college, but as yet there is nothing more. Whether it will vanish or continue, time alone can determine.

With affection & respect
Yours truly
A. GREEN.

REVD. DR. JAMES RICHARDS,
   New Ark,
      New Jersey.

o'clock the tremendous explosion took place of what has been denominated the *big cracker.*" At two o'clock that morning the outbuildings of the college were discovered to be on fire. The steward, with the aid of the tutors and some orderly students, extinguished the flames so quickly that the greater part of the college knew nothing of it. In the morning it appeared that arrangements had been made "for some mighty work of mischief" in the Prayer Hall. Loose powder, a quantity of tinder, and a keg were found on the stage of the hall before the pulpit. The intention had evidently been to divert attention by the conflagration outside, and then spring the mine within. The day passed quietly, however, until about nine o'clock, when a tremendous crash shook the entire building. The President, who was walking in his study at the time, hastened to the scene. In the second entry he found the remains of an "infernal machine," which had been constructed from the huge hub of a wagon wheel, loaded with several pounds of powder. The adjacent walls were cracked from top to bottom, nearly all the glass in the vicinity was broken, and a large piece of the bomb had been driven through the door of the Prayer Hall. The President acted with so much vigor and judgment in discovering and punishing the perpetrators that he had no serious trouble afterwards.

I cannot resist the temptation to quote one little incident from his autobiography, which throws a curious light on the primitive methods of discipline in the days when there was no Mat. Goldie,* armed with the terrors of a proctor's authority:

"At length, however, the disorder was extended to the entries of the college. When this took place I, on a certain evening, took a candle in my hand, and went to the passage through which the mass of students return from supper. They passed me in perfect silence and respect; but as soon as they got out of sight in the upper entries, some of them began the usual yell. The vice-president ran through the crowd and seized one of the small rogues in the very act of clapping and hallooing, took him up in his arms, and brought him through the whole corps, and set him down before me, as I stood with the candle in my hand, talking to a crowd that I had called about me. I seized the opportunity to address them at some length, and to endeavor to reason, to shame, and to intimidate them out of their folly. . . . It certainly had a good effect."

The close of the college year witnessed another interesting scene on the commencement stage. Winfield Scott, still suffering from the glorious wounds of war, was passing through

* College proctor from 1870-1892.

Princeton on his way from the north. He was borne to the platform, where "all united in clamorous greetings to the young, wounded soldier, the only representative that they had seen of a successful, noble army." The valedictorian had taken as his theme, "A Patriot Citizen in Time of War." By permission of the Faculty, changes were made which gave it a personal reference, and the future Major-General was able to understand how Washington felt under a similar ordeal, thirty-one years before.

The commencement of that day had a picturesque accompaniment, which reminds one of an old harvest festival in Merrie Englande. The crops were all garnered, and the country folk for miles around flocked to the town to see the distinguished visitors and celebrate the end of another season's toil. The street in front of the college and the church where commencement exercises were held resembled a county fair. Hundreds of men, women, and children surrounded the booths, tables, and wagons, where venders praised the virtues of their cheap wares, or comforted the crowd with cider and small beer. At intervals the street was rapidly cleared, and tumultuous cheers greeted a bunch of panting horses as they dashed down the highway for the local sweepstakes. Boys and men played for

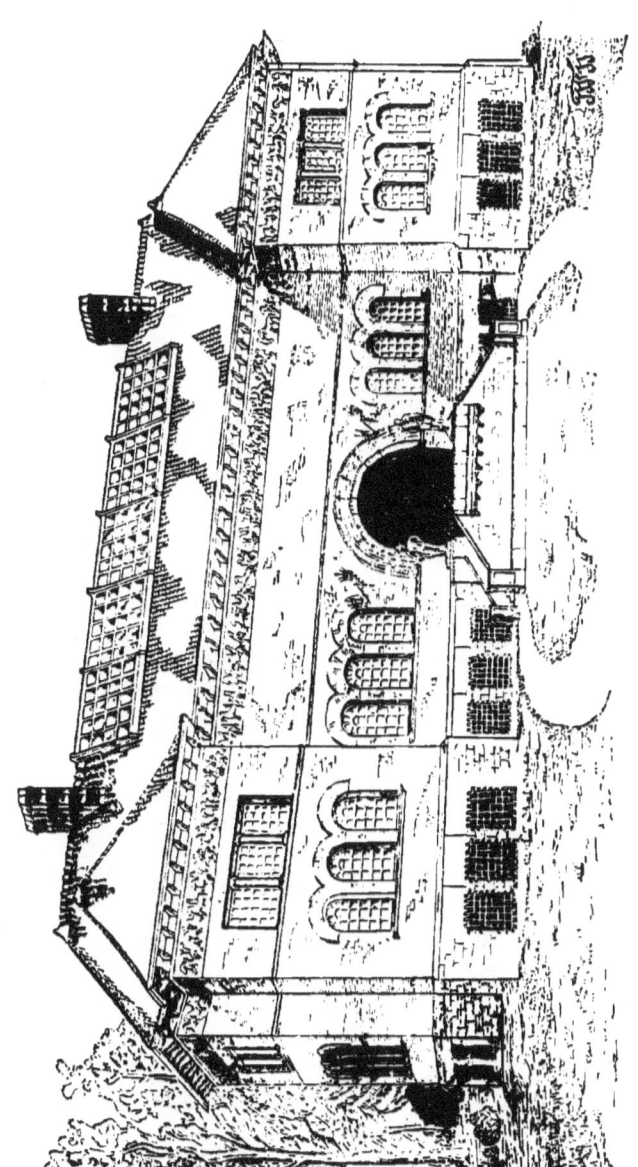

MUSEUM OF HISTORIC ART.

pennies, fiddlers scraped away while robust couples danced the country jigs. On one occasion the venerable old cannon back of North was forced to be party to a bull-baiting. The unfortunate brute was fastened by the horns to the Revolutionary veteran, and worried by a pack of dogs, to the great delectation of a large and appreciative assemblage.

This annual saturnalia was naturally excessively annoying to the college authorities, and so early as 1807 we find the Board passing the following resolution :

"*Resolved*, That no person whatever be permitted to erect any booth, or fix any wagon for selling liquor or other refreshment on the day of Commencement on the ground of the College, except on that part of the road to the eastward of the middle gate of the front Campus, and that this Board will pay the expense of carrying this resolution into effect."

It was largely in order to escape these "unhappy accompaniments," that the day for commencement was changed, in 1843, from September to the month of June.

If it is true that the nation is happy which has no history, Princeton men can look with pleasure on the thirty years of Dr. James Carnahan's presidency, extending from 1823 to 1853. The record of this period is a record of prosperity and quiet, substantial growth. East and West colleges, a professor's house, a refectory, a chapel, and the Whig and Clio Halls were built. The campus was enlarged and improved, the standard of studies gradually raised, and the number of instructors tripled.

The administration of President Maclean "the best loved man in America," was marked by two unfortunate events: the burning of Nassau Hall in 1855, and the withdrawal of the Southern students at the beginning of the war.

Princeton had always an unusually large constituency in the South—more so than any other Northern institution. In ante-bellum days about two fifths of the undergraduates were from that section. Naturally the intense political feeling of the time found its expression among the students, and heated discussions often led to arguments of a different kind. A national flag which had been run up over the belfry of Old North was taken down by order of the President. The Faculty, although thoroughly loyal to the Union, endeavored to keep the peace of the college by preventing conflicts which might lead to disorder. The Northern men insisted on the flag, however, and Capt. John Margerum of Princeton, amid the enthusiastic cheers of the students, climbed to the dizzy height above the

WIN COLLEGE

cupola and fastened the old colors to the topmost peak. The flag was hardly up, before a heavy gale bent the rod, so that the vane pointed to the north throughout the four years of the war. This reminiscence is still cherished by old citizens as one of the omens of the time. Three students, who had been expelled for "pumping" a too outspoken "copperhead," were sent away with a grand demonstration. Enthroned in a wagon, bedecked with flags and banners, they were drawn through the town by hundreds of citizens and students, who tugged at the long ropes and heralded their approach by tumultuous cheering. Numerous stops were made, and the long serpent which drew the car circled again about it, to shout themselves hoarse over the speeches of the retiring patriots.

After Sumter was fired on, the Southern students—more than ninety in number—withdrew in a body, and the perplexities of the Faculty were at an end.

President Maclean carried the college through the troublous times which followed, and retired in 1868, beloved by all his students, and venerated by all who knew him. During his term, gifts amounting to more than $400,000 were bestowed upon the college, the Halsted Observatory was secured, and the splendid foundation of the John C. Green School of Science projected. The third and most glorious era had begun, and it remained for Dr. McCosh to realize its magnificent promise, and add his name to the list of brilliant men who have presided over the destinies of Nassau Hall.

V.

ADMINISTRATION OF JAMES McCOSH.

It was a good day for Princeton when Dr. McCosh wrote from Queen's College, Belfast:

"I devote myself and my remaining life, under God, to old Princeton, and the religious and literary interests with which it is identified, and, I fancy, will leave my bones in your graveyard beside the great and good men who are buried there, hoping that my spirit may mount to communion with them in heaven."

Dr. McCosh's early life was spent on his father's farm, in the southern part of Ayrshire. Here he was reared in a thatched dwelling, surrounded by cow-houses, a stable, cart-house, and barn. This modest home looked out upon the smiling valley of the Doon, and over the meadows and hills of the "land of Burns" the farmer's boy was accustomed to wander at will with his pony, "Cuddy," and his collie, "Famous," studying the meadow-sweet and foxglove, observing the habits of birds, and exercising that reflective disposition which he had inherited from his father.

In November, 1824, an Ayrshire boy, age thirteen, was entered in the preparatory class at Glasgow University. He was a tall, shy youth, and his fellow collegians took little or no notice of him. He made few friends, and lived the retired and uneventful life of a student. The languages he acquired with difficulty, but early in his course the fascinating problems of philosophy took possession of his mind. He had also an insatiable appetite for miscellaneous reading, devoured the works of Scott and Byron as they came out, and roused the anger of a somewhat choleric librarian by insisting on having new books immediately upon their publication. His mind developed slowly, and, owing to his extreme youth, he did not succeed in surpassing the leading students, although maintaining an honorable rank. He left Glasgow, he says, without a professor or fellow-student imagining that he would ever reach any distinction. He was a Scotchman, and could keep his own counsel, but built into the rugged granite of his character was the unexpressed thought and purpose that "I would one day hold my place with the best of them, provided perseverance could do it."

PRESIDENT McCOSH.

In the fall of 1829 James McCosh, drawn by the name of Thomas Chalmers, went to Edinburgh, where he pursued a divinity course for five years. The personal force of this great teacher, the richness of his thought and the impetuosity of his eloquence, made a deep impression on the student from Glasgow, and in later life he expressed the opinion that Chalmers was, upon the whole, the greatest man he had met with. Those were the golden days of Edinburgh, when John Leslie and Sir William Hamilton were delivering their lectures, when the redoubtable Francis Jeffrey was training the guns of the *Edinburgh Review*, and "the great unknown" was entertaining the world with his Waverley Novels. Edinburgh did not require as much commonplace daily study as Glasgow, but the atmosphere of the place was literary and philosophical, and under its genial influence the ripening powers of the future metaphysician began to show their real vigor.

Mr. McCosh had been in the university a very short time, before his abilities were recognized and he won and maintained a high rank and an influential position among the students. The new science of geology interested him greatly; he read deeply in philosophy, and, at times, in fact, gave his theological studies a rather subordinate place. After completing his course he shrank from entering the ministry at once, doubting his fitness, and devoted another year to reading.

In the spring of 1834 he was finally licensed by the Presbytery of Ayr, a member being appointed to tell him he must make his preaching more popular and less abstract, leaving out such phrases as *transcendental* and the like,—an admonition which the young minister endeavored patiently and successfully to obey. This is not the place to give an account of Dr. McCosh's long and eventful service in the ministry, his various pastorates, and his fearless leadership in fighting Establishment and founding the Free Church of Scotland. In 1850 he published his *Method of Divine Government*, a book which has gone through at least twenty editions, and which at once established his reputation as a writer and thinker.

The year 1852 saw him installed as Professor of Logic and Metaphysics at Queens College, Belfast. For sixteen years he devoted himself to teaching and research in those fields of knowledge to which his genius called him, writing a number of books, and throwing himself eagerly into the philosophical battles of the time. In the midst of this active and absorbing

McCOSH WALK.

life, he came home, one May evening, from his work in Queens, and found a despatch announcing that he had been elected President of Princeton College.

Before the election of Dr. McCosh the students were unanimously in his favor, and when, on the 20th of October, 1868, the *Tripoli* was reported off Sandy Hook, they were prepared to give the newly arrived President a rousing reception.

In the words of the *Lit.* "Gossip" of that time:

"As the hands of the clock crept around to four, there arose from the college a shout, the Nassau shout, which always draws a crowd. Then there was a rushing to the depot, and a marshalling of students. Soon the shrill whistle, and after, the 'down brakes,' announced that he had come—announced THE ARRIVAL OF McCOSH. Of course there was cheering again, the old cheer of the Nassaus, and the procession moved towards the President's house. . . . Arrived at the house, the students formed in semi-circle about the front, when Dr. Atwater, Acting President, introduced to them Their Real President, JAMES McCOSH. He, stepping forth, was received with loudest hurrahing."

That night the Triangle resounded to the tread of marching columns, rockets shot up into the night, and the old cannon glowed red to its very heart, under the roar of a blazing bonfire. A week later, the inauguration. Everybody is here. The new President is welcomed by polished addresses in English and a learned speech in Latin. That evening the campus is gay with flaring calcium lights and the mellower rays of colored transparencies for the first time since the visit of Lafayette.

Dr. McCosh's long experience as a teacher, his important service in developing the University of Belfast, and his intimate acquaintance with the educational methods of Europe and America, gave him a special fitness for the task with which he was confronted. His first report to the Board of Trustees indicated that a strong hand was upon the helm. Among the eight recommendations he offered, are two of special significance.

The first was that " Encouragement should be given to the founding of scholarships or fellowships, to be earned by graduates at a competition and fitted to promote high scholarship, and retain young men of ability for a longer time at their favorite studies." It was the President's opinion that the attainments of the great majority of students was as high in America as in Europe. But he found in the new world no selected body of men doing post-graduate work along special lines and cultivating a high grade of scholarship.

It was to meet this need that the recommendation was made. As a result, there are now a dozen fellowships in various departments offered to the graduating class, and the remarkable roll of scholars and professors who have been graduated under Dr. McCosh, shows how successful his policy has been.

The second recommendation concerned the introduction of electives. In 1868 the candidates for degrees were confined to a four-years' required course in Latin, Greek, and mathematics, with a little science and philosophy. It was felt that some place should be found for the new studies which the great advances in science had developed, and at the same time the degrees must not be suffered to lose their meaning. It was found impossible to require additional studies while retaining all old ones, and the elective system was devised to meet the difficulty. During the twenty years of his administration, this elective system was carefully matured, under the judicious and progressive direction of the President. Step by step, the number of electives was increased, until required work in classics and mathematics became confined to freshman and sophomore years, and the upper classmen could make their choice from an inviting schedule, containing as great a number of branches as are usually taught in the universities of England, Scotland, and Ireland, and nearly all the branches taught in Germany.

The spirit of Dr. McCosh's administration is well expressed in a sentence or two from his closing address:

"I said to myself and I said to others, We have a fine old college here, with many friends ; why should we not make it equal to any college in America, and, in the end, to any in Europe ? The friends of Princeton saw I was in earnest, and nobly did they encourage me."

"In those days I was like the hound in the leash ready to start, and they encouraged me with their shouts as I sprang forth to the hunt."

The enthusiasm was contagious. The students talked of the "new era," and generous alumni responded liberally to the Doctor's calls for funds. Money poured in. New chairs were endowed, and buildings went up as if by magic.

There has scarcely been a time since 1868 when some part of the campus has not been littered with the stones and lumber of a new building. The Halsted Observatory was rising when Dr. McCosh was inaugurated. In his speech on that occasion, the incoming President declared

THE SCHOOL OF SCIENCE.

with great applause from the students, that every college should have a gymnasium for the body as well as for the mind. It was not two years before he had the pleasure of dedicating what was then the best gymnasium in America. Shortly afterwards, Dickinson Hall was opened with its comfortable recitation rooms. In 1871 Reunion Hall added a dormitory for the rapidly increasing number of students. Two years later the Chancellor Green Library was completed. In the same year Mr. J. C. Green started the Quadrangle of the School of Science, the stately Gothic façade of which ornaments the eastern campus. Then followed Murray Hall, devoted to the use of the Philadelphian Society. In rapid succession University Hall, Witherspoon, the new President's Mansion, Marquand Chapel, Edwards Hall, The Biological Museum, and the Art School were added, not to mention some less imposing buildings.

Before the rapid multiplication of buildings had gone far, a landscape gardener was employed to prepare a plan for the extension and improvement of the campus. Dr. McCosh took a great interest in this work, and had the grounds laid out somewhat on the model of the demesnes of English noblemen. Dozens of deformed trees and shrubs bowed to his orders, and hundreds of new ones were planted under his directions. On more than one uncertain April day has the tall form of the President been seen on the campus, as he walked about with shoots and cuttings under his arm, carefully deciding where they should be placed. The contrasting styles and architectural beauty of the new buildings were well set off by the smooth sweep of shady lawns between, and the result is a campus which was some years ago pronounced by the President of Harvard the most beautiful in America.

This material development was paralleled by not less extensive additions to the teaching force. In 1868 there were ten professors, four tutors, two teachers, in all sixteen engaged in instruction, besides three extraordinary lecturers. In enlarging the teaching corps, as demanded by the expanding curriculum and the growing number of students, it was found difficult to secure the kind of men desired. A system of training professors was accordingly introduced. College Fellows were started as tutors and instructors, finally working into full professorships. As a result of this method, nearly all the younger members of the faculty are Princeton men. In 1888, the teaching force consisted of thirty-five professors, three tutors, and

THE FRONT CAMPUS.

several assistants and lecturers, in all upwards of forty.

Dr. McCosh criticised the European universities for their utter neglect of students outside of the class-room. He felt that, without in any way infringing on the liberty of students, it was possible to take an interest in their welfare, and come into contact with them in a personal way. It was his determined policy to endeavor to impress upon the incoming professors, a sense of their responsibility in this direction. The kindly Doctor was not content with enforcing regulations for the preservation of college morals. He opened his doors and received the students with unstinted hospitality into his spacious mansion. Many an alumnus cherishes in his memory a picture of that tea-table, a few students around it, the Doctor at the head, leading the conversation with his strong, cheery voice and slight Scotch accent; his wife Isabella, "the mother of the students," opposite him, pouring tea and making friendly inquiries.

What student of the last administration does not remember Isabella McCosh? No undergraduate could be sick for a day without hearing her gentle rap at his door; without receiving the benediction of that sweet, motherly face, and enjoying the light ministrations of her hands. Appetizing broths, and delicacies in snowy napkins came over from Prospect, and it is feared that occasionally a homesick student found it pleasanter to be on the sick-list under the jurisdiction of Mrs. McCosh than on the roll of active service under the professors. And when the beautiful infirmary which now graces the hill-crest on the campus was first projected, it could have received no other name than that which it now bears: "The Isabella McCosh Infirmary."

There were some matters of discipline requiring attention, and the new President took hold of them with a prudent yet vigorous hand. Hazing in particular was at that time a general practice, and was carried at times to almost brutal extremes. On one memorable occasion a freshman was observed in chapel with a smooth and shining expanse of head that would have rivalled the display of the baldest octogenarian. The President sent for Chancellor Green and took legal advice. The prospect of a criminal action and a course in the State prison brought the offenders to their knees. They all confessed, promised never to do it again, and were pardoned. The result of such a course was a vast abatement of the evil. In fact, after a few years scarcely any hazing was practised, if we except a little harmless "guying" on the campus.

In the early '70's it was found necessary to take measures against the Greek-letter fraternities. Although under the ban of college law, they had gradually worked their way in, and finally were openly avowed, by the display of badges upon the campus. In their train came disaster to the two old literary halls. At that time the representative orators and debaters were chosen, not by contest, as at present, but by popular election. The fraternity men in the halls intrigued for their own men, literary qualifications were largely overlooked, and the institutions were becoming reduced to disorderly lobbies. Literary life was dying out. The halls took the question up themselves, and became divided into two warring factions—the fraternity and the anti-fraternity men.

The influence of these organizations extended outside of the halls. They conspired to protect their men from discipline, and on one occasion a single suspension was followed by an open outbreak. Under these circumstances the President threw his heavy sword into the scales of the anti-fraternity men. There was vigorous opposition from the hostile faction and great excitement throughout the college, but fraternities had to go, root and branch. Rid of this disintegrating element, Whig and Clio revived, the college recovered its ancient spirit of unity, and now the most pronounced enemies of fraternities are the students themselves.

Possibly this chapter would not be complete without some reference to the "Cannon War" with Rutgers. By some process, not exactly understood, the Rutgers boys came to believe that the smaller of the two cannon left here after the battle of Princeton belonged to them. Accordingly, in the spring vacation of 1875, when the campus was deserted, a large force from New Brunswick made a night raid upon Princeton, dislodged the object of attack by a vigorous onslaught of picks and shovels, and with great valor carried their trophy back to Rutgers.

When the spring vacation was over, and only a hole in the ground was found in place of the cherished totem, great was the wrath among the Nassaus. A campaign was organized at once, and a long column set out for the banks of the Raritan, breathing out threatenings and slaughter. The cannon had been too safely secreted, but a museum in connection with the college was taken, and some old muskets carried back by way of reprisal. At this point diplomacy intervened. The

ON THE CAMPUS.—VIEW FROM PROSPECT.

ardor of the combatants was restrained, while the two Faculties appointed committees to look into the matter. Of course, an examination of the records could lead to only one decision. The relic was brought back and planted again with appropriate ceremonies; long iron rods were twisted around it and embedded deeply in cement to prevent a repetition of the theft, and the temple of Janus was closed.

At the commencement of 1888 Dr. McCosh surrendered the keys which he had held for twenty years. It was a deeply impressive sight to see that tall and rugged figure, that massive head fringed with locks of white, that strongly featured face furrowed with the lines of thought and shining with the light of a gracious soul, as the retiring President told the story of "Twenty Years of Princeton College," and transferred the responsibility of his beloved college to another.

"I take the step," he says, "firmly and decidedly. The shadows are lengthening, the day is declining. My age, seven years above the threescore and ten, compels it, Providence points to it, conscience enjoins it, the good of the college demands it. I take the step as one of duty. I feel relieved as I take it."

The mantle of Elijah has fallen upon Elisha.

While we leave the college in the hands of another, let us take a look at the venerable ex-President in the home of his old age on Prospect Avenue. The large bow windows of his library look over forty miles of rolling Jersey woods and meadow-land to the blue line of the Navesink Highlands. Here he has employed his time in revising the more important of his published works. That task completed, his active mind resents the increasing infirmities of age, and demands some employment. His mind turns to the past, and his indefatigable pen is busy upon a series of sketches entitled "*Incidents of My Life in Three Countries.*" This task also is finished. If we would learn the spirit of the man and receive a parting benediction from his venerable hands, let us look over his shoulder, as his pen traces the words of the closing soliloquy:

"Farewell, hill and dale, mountain and valley, fountain and stream, river and brook, lake and outflow, forest and shady dell, sun and moon, earth and sky. I have lived among you, I have been closely acquainted with you, I have watched you and your aspects and wandered much among you, I have delighted in you and loved you, and my heart lingers among you. I feel that there is nothing wrong in this, for I know that ye are all the works of God. Ye may have been defiled by the deeds of men, but ye are yourselves chaste. The air that breathes from you is pure and exhilarating ; I will not forget you. In my everlasting existence I may hope to revisit you and renew my ardor.

"Welcome, what immeasurably exceeds all these—Heaven with its glory! Heaven with its angels that excel in strength ! Heaven with the spirits of just men made perfect! Heaven with Jesus Himself so full of tenderness ! Heaven with Father, Son, and Holy Ghost."

VI.

PRINCETON UNIVERSITY.

In President McCosh's closing address, he said:

"I think it proper to state that I meant all along that these new and varied studies, with their groupings and combinations, should lead to the formation of a *studium generale*, which was supposed in the Middle Ages to constitute a university. At one time I cherished the hope that I might be honored to introduce such a measure. From my intimate acquaintance with the systems of Princeton and other colleges, I was so vain as to think that out of our available materials I could have constructed a university of a high order. . . . The college has been brought to the very borders, and I leave it to another to carry it over into the land of promise."

In this country particularly, the term university is used with a vast amount of latitude. In the absence of any legal or definite historical criterion, the name has been used without careful discrimination, and has, in many cases, been appropriated by institutions which are clearly beyond the pale of any definition, however generous, their only justification being an ambition to some day deserve the title. In Europe, new institutions are not nearly so numerous. The older seats of learning hold this name by a well-earned prescription, and even where new schools are started, an instinctive conservatism prevents the hasty assumption of university rank.

The tendency in America seems to be to reserve the strict use of the term for institutions which have the four faculties: arts, law, medicine, and theology; but history does not justify this limitation. Salerno, Bologna, and Paris were universities when they had but one faculty.

It is thought by others that a curriculum offering a wide range of studies, with freedom of choice to the student body, constitutes a university. But, since there is no one to say just where the line must be drawn as to extent of courses and freedom of choice, the definition is of little practical value. The English universities are merely examining and degree-granting bodies, with more or less closely affiliated colleges under them. But, judged by this standard, many of the foremost universities of the world must abandon their claim to that distinction. The German conception seems to be that a university is an institution designed to promote original research and encourage the work of specialists. It would seem, then, that, historically, this title has been applied to seats of learning which, either by the wide range of courses offered, or by a particularly high standard of excellence in special departments, have crossed a certain indefinable line, and won for themselves a position in the first rank of learning. Judged, either by the number of her faculties, the extent of her courses, the freedom of choice offered to the students, or the cultivation of original research by a picked body of specialists, Princeton is certainly a university, in the strictest sense, if there is one in this country.

As to the particular kind of university which Princeton represents, it may be said that her type is composite. The founders of the College of New Jersey designed it upon the broad basis of a *studium generale*. Their expressed purpose was an opportunity for liberal culture. The subsequent expansion has resulted from natural and healthy evolution. By steadily raising the entrance requirements, and extending the curriculum under the elective system, the Faculty of Arts has been brought to a position where juniors and seniors are doing real university work.

BRONZE STATUE OF PRESIDENT McCOSH IN MARQUAND CHAPEL.

The School of Science was originally founded to find a place for the sciences which were clamoring for admission into the regular academic course. It was not designed to give a merely technical training, but to satisfy the demand for a course which would recognize, to the fullest extent, the disciplinary value of modern scientific studies. Modern languages took the place of classics, and some of the English and other courses of the Academic Department were required, in order that the first conception of the college, a broad, humanizing culture, might not yield to a narrow, technical training.

The development of the school, however, and its greatest success has been along lines other than those anticipated by its founders. It has grown with amazing rapidity, and its requirements have been steadily raised. Courses are offered, with a liberal range of electives, in general science, chemistry, and biology and chemistry, for a degree of bachelor of science. There are also courses for degrees of Civil Engineer and Electrical Engineer. A minority of the students in the school, however, have entered for the general Bachelor of Science course, sixty per cent. of the undergraduates enrolled being candidates for the degrees of

C.E. or E.E. This tendency has been recognized by the Scientific Faculty; courses have been adapted; the best apparatus and equipment have been put at the service of technical students, and the result is that a large body of men are graduated every year, prepared to enter at once upon the practice of their professions.

The School of Science has already evolved two separate schools of the first rank. The new chemical laboratory was designed by Prof. Cornwall, after a careful study of the leading schools at home and abroad. The result is a building which, for convenience and completeness of equipment, is at present unrivalled. Beside the regular undergraduates, there is an increasing number of graduate students who are doing advanced and special work of a high order.

The new Electrical School, under Prof. Brackett, has also the advantage of a thoroughly modern equipment. Most of its students have already taken the first degree, either in arts or science, and the course is thoroughly technical, with severe requirements both in the theory and practice of electrical engineering.

Princeton has no undue ambition to multiply her faculties. The opportunities of her present field are felt to be so vast, that her main energies may well be directed in conserving and devel-

THE DYNAMO HOUSE.

oping what is already here. The tendency seems to be for each department to grow into a more advanced university type, acquiring, as it develops, something of an autonomy. In the Academic School, the Departments of Philosophy, Language and Literature, and Mathematics and Natural Science have already made considerable progress in the direction of advanced work by post-graduate specialists. In addition to the fourteen university fellows, there are now over a hundred graduate students in the various courses, seventy per cent. of whom have taken the first degree in other colleges.

There is, of course, no Theological Faculty, the Princeton Seminary having no organic connection whatever with the college. This is doubtless an advantage, since a seminary can hardly escape a denominational character, while a university must, of course, be entirely free from such limitations. At the same time there is a friendly reciprocity which secures all the substantial advantages of an organic union. The students of each institution are admitted freely to the courses of the other, and the privileges of both libraries are also enjoyed in common.

Perhaps the next development will be in the direction of a Law Faculty. It is one of the President's most cherished projects, and will doubtless be realized as soon as the necessary funds are available. It is not his design to establish a law school in the ordinary sense of the term—that is to say, a school to prepare men merely for their bar examinations. Dr. Patton wishes to found chairs from which law will be taught, not so much as a science as a branch of philosophy. The professional law schools have no time to deal with the History and Philosophy of Jurisprudence, and the institution which first secures a foundation for advanced study in this department will enter a field comparatively unoccupied in this country, and will doubtless draw about it a select body of scholarly jurists. Experience has shown that such a philosophical course affords an invaluable basis for the subsequent study of practice law. This Law School will not come as a creation, but as the outgrowth of the present Department in Political Science. In fact, it is in a measure already realized.

When Dr. McCosh came to Princeton, the catalogue showed 264 students; when he retired, the number enrolled had increased to 603. Dr. Patton in his inaugural was rash enough to express the hope that he might live to see the numbers reach 1000. Four years have sufficed to see his dream more than

THE MAGNETIC OBSERVATORY.

realized, and the only practical limit to growth seems to be the lack of accommodations. During this period twelve buildings have been erected or undertaken at an aggregate cost of over $1,000,000, and other valuable endowments have been given to the college. However, the needs have outstripped the generosity of friends, most of the recent structures have increased the expenses rather than the revenues, and there was never a time when liberal endowments were more urgently required. About thirty men have been added to the teaching force, and the strain upon resources in this regard is particularly severe.

This unprecedented growth, so inspiring to all who are interested in Old Nassau, is due to a variety of causes.

A large part of it is a direct outgrowth of the splendid work done under the administration of Dr. McCosh. His own world-wide reputation strengthened the college he governed. Under his leadership, Trustees, Faculty, alumni, and students were united in an earnest effort to push Princeton into the foremost place, and a number of wealthy benefactors came forward to make the accomplishment of their plans possible. The country at large is just beginning to realize what Princeton has become, and the natural result is a great increase in the number of applications for matriculation.

When Dr. Patton took the presidential chair, he was known as a man of profound erudition and brilliant intellectual gifts. During the four years of his administration, he has shown himself as skilful and successful in dealing with the executive details of his office, as in handling the more abstruse questions of metaphysics. The charm of his personality, and his sparkling addresses, have won the hearts of alumni all over the country. Most of all, perhaps, his generous confidence in the student body, his ready sympathy with undergraduate life, and the kindly interest he shows in all whose affairs may require his consideration, have won for him the steadfast regard of every man on the campus. The first requisite to the growth of such an institution is enthusiasm, and there was never a more enthusiastic body of men than those who are at present supporting the President in his labors for advancing the university.

Princeton has also a cosmopolitan character, not enjoyed in the same degree by many of her rivals. Of course, the convenience of neighborhood gives to every institution a large local *clientèle*, and two-thirds of the students at Nassau come from the four great Middle

THE HALSTED OBSERVATORY.

States. It must be remembered, however, that this territory represents an area of over one hundred thousand square miles. Of the remaining students, 17 per cent. come from the Western States, 12 per cent. from the South, 1 per cent. from New England, and 4 per cent. from foreign countries. During recent years, the rapid gains from the West and South have been particularly noticeable. In ante-bellum days one third of the degrees were granted to Southern students, and there is scarcely a great family in all that region that cannot point to its name recurring more than once in the Catalogus Collegii Neo-Cæsariensis. The prostration that followed the war, and the almost total extermination of many leading families, affected Princeton's roll very seriously; but with the present revival of material interests in the South, her sons are beginning to return to their historic Mater, and the last five years have doubled the representation from that section.

The shifting of the centre of population toward the west is also giving Princeton an increasing advantage over her ancient rivals. Situated on the great trunk line of the country, and midway between the two commercial capitals of the Atlantic Coast, she occupies a strategic position destined to give her a constantly increasing hold upon the great regions which lie toward the setting sun.

It is not strange, in view of the brilliant past of the old college, and the marvellous renaissance which recent years have witnessed, that Princeton men should look towards the future with unhesitating confidence and enthusiasm. They are proverbially the most devoted body of collegians in the country. With an ardor which time does not seem to diminish, gray-haired alumni unite with undergraduates in chanting the praises of the present, and prophesying great things to be written upon the virgin pages of coming years. The critical observer will doubtless make some deductions for the pardonable optimism which springs from a deep, personal interest. At the same time, he will recognize that a great enthusiasm cannot come without some adequate exciting cause. He will see that an institution which wins such allegiance from her sons must possess an atmosphere most favorable to the development of a generous, manly culture; he will perceive in the spirit which pervades the sons of Nassau Hall, the strongest justification of her present claims, as well as find in it the surest indication of a fondly anticipated destiny.

THE WOKING OBSERVATORY.

VII.

UNDER THE PRINCETON ELMS.

These old elms on the campus know more than they tell. Very few rushes they have not seen; not a cane-spree but they have caught glimpses of it around the corners of West College; they have stood about the bonfires in the Quadrangle at many a great celebration, and have cast their shadows on groups of men saddened by touch-downs at the wrong end of the field. If Nassau Hall has a familiar spirit, and it certainly must have, you may be quite sure that it is lurking somewhere among the branches of the old elms. Without them Princeton would not be Princeton.

At Northfield recently, where over one hundred and twenty colleges were represented, an Oberlin man remarked how the Princeton boys seemed to stick together. "Why," he said, "you fellows are just like one big family." And he was right. There is no other college of the size where the undergraduates are so well acquainted. It was in Princeton that the college grounds were first called The Campus, and it is in Princeton only that the full meaning of the word is realized. How we do like to talk about that old Campus, with its broad stretches of lawn, its stately buildings and venerable elms! How we love to breathe its air and revel in its unlimited freedom! How often have we thrown down our books and sought relief for weary brain in its inexhaustible resources! Does any one wish a little practice at his favorite sport? Let him go out on the Campus and meet a lot of fellows looking for the same thing. Does he want a companion for a walk, or a party for a quiet game in his room? He can find them on the Campus. Does he long for the pleasure of a pure and simple loaf? He may join the groups in front of Old North and forget the ills of life in the careless drift of college chat. One can't help getting acquainted. Yale and Harvard men have told me that they have gone through their course knowing only a dozen or so men. Nearly every man here is acquainted with his whole class, and is on speaking terms with half the college. Our dormitories are nothing but big club-houses, and the Campus is simply an extension built out into the open air.

UNDER THE ELMS.

Then the eating clubs. They are generally made up of a dozen or more congenial fellows who make arrangements with the powers of the kitchen through an agent or "club runner." The club runner is the Tribune of the People, and it is his business to present the complaints and wishes of his clients to the portly landlady (all Princeton landladies are portly), who is invariably on the brink of ruin because she gives her boarders too much for the money. If the Tribune cannot preserve the comity of gastronomic relations, he takes his club to another house, which is always "the best place in town." These little circles around the table are the units of college life. They are the little forums where everything is discussed, from football to the Kantian Critique; in their daily pow-wows friendships are formed which will never be broken. They are made up of men of kindred tastes, and each one has its distinctive character. One club in the senior class is composed entirely of philosophers. Go there for dinner, and you will see everybody forgetting his soup until they have settled the relative merits of Calderwood's and Martineau's theories of the conscience. It would not be hard to find other clubs where conscience never interferes with the soup.

Twice within the last fifteen years has a "Commons" been established, where excellent food was supplied at reasonable rates. But each time the boys soon pined for the privacy and freedom of the old club-room with its song and jest, and the commons became a thing of the past. In recent years many of the clubs have become more ambitious, and a number of commodious houses have been erected. Here the dining-room and back parlor of the village houses have given place to all the comforts of a modern club. *Ivy* was the first to build. Already the inviting homes of *Cap and Gown, Cottage, Colonial, Tiger Inn,* and *University* are occupied by their members, and additional buildings are going up every year.

If the social life at Princeton is not remarkably gay, it is exceedingly pleasant. The winter brings on the Senior Assembly and the Junior Promenade with their accompanying teas, and the Sophomore Reception makes a gala night in the middle of commencement week. Each Friday evening finds a procession of pilgrims on their way to the weekly reception at Evelyn, and orange-and-black buttons are often seen in New York, Philadelphia, and Trenton drawing-rooms. Princeton is one of the oldest towns in Jersey, and is still the residence of a

number of colonial families, whose homesteads give an added charm to the quiet streets, and whose modern representatives unite with the professors and their families to make up "Princeton society." This circle is, of course, quite small in proportion to the size of the college, but the Princeton people throw open their doors with a hospitality which goes far to compensate for lack of numbers.

There are always some men who go out considerably, and if the number is not as large as it might be, the students have only themselves to blame. The fact is, our college life is so full and absorbing, that there is little inclination to supplement it. After running around in flannels all day, the decision is generally one way when the alternative comes in the evening of attiring one's self for a call or dropping into a neighbor's room. Who does not know the charm of those evenings in a fellow's room? It does n't matter much what is done. A few banjos improvise an orchestra; there are stories, songs, jests, a hand at whist; possibly crackers and cider for refreshments. The details are of small importance; the real pleasure is in the freedom and abandon of college companionship, the jolly *camaraderie* of half a dozen of the best fellows in the world.

These little circles fill many a long winter evening, but when the spring comes the twang of the banjo is low, and the thud of the base-ball bat is heard in the land. Everybody moves outside and becomes an athlete. The *Princetonian* issues its annual challenge to the *Lit.*; eating-club teams organize and train with an ardor worthy of the 'Varsity, and every other man you meet is a captain or manager. He is looking for another captain or manager, and wants to arrange a game for that afternoon back of Witherspoon. A good-natured crowd is on hand to coach, cheer, or guy, as the occasion demands, while the "Grasshoppers" hammer out base hits on the "Hoffman House," or the "Butterflies" make life miserable for the umpire. One can't live in Princeton without learning to play ball. On a good spring day you can scarcely walk from Reunion to the gymnasium without having to field a ball gone astray from some bat, to which your attention is called by vociferous cries of "Thank you, there!" In the fall it is football, and wonderful teams in a wonderful medley of costumes play with the desperation of a Thanksgiving game.

Then those Saturday trips to the neighboring preparatory schools! It is a beautiful day;

THE BROKAW MEMORIAL BUILDING AND SWIMMING TANK.

coaches, overflowing with players, managers, and mascots, leave the front campus gate after dinner, and spin across the country to Lawrenceville, Hightstown, or Pennington. The "preps" always labor under the impression that they are playing, if not the 'Varsity, at least the 'Varsity scrub, and a corresponding degree of enthusiasm prevails. The girls are out on the grand stand in full force, and applaud fine catches and errors with delightful impartiality. If the visitors lose, they leave a proud and happy prep. school behind them; but little care they for that. Their coach rolls back to Princeton over the moonlit road, their jolly chorus wakes the plodding Jersey farmer, and it is midnight when some strolling students hail them at the campus gate with, "What's the score?"

There is an impression among many who have never seen university life from the inside, that the good old days when men studied have gone by, and the porches of the academe have yielded to the shining track of Olympia. Twenty years ago there were no college athletics, and now the outside world hears of little else. Thirty thousand people go to the great games in New York; only the night watchman sees the light in the window burning late into the night, where some Sophomore is wrestling with conic sections, or a belated Senior is pouring over the mysteries of the *ens realissimum*. The New York papers print long articles on the sprinter who breaks the world's record in the hundred yards, and publish portraits of the famous half-backs. No one sees how these same men toil for literary and curriculum honors when they leave the athletic field; no mention is made of their twelve hundred college mates who are quietly earning their degree by four years' honest work. Indeed there is a vast amount of intellectual life outside of the regular courses. The two Halls are filled with eager debaters and orators. Shakespeare clubs, and all manner of literary circles meet during the winter, and spend long hours in settling the great problems of literary controversy. Three periodicals are supported by the college and entirely conducted by undergraduates.

At the same time this is not what we care to talk about. Hours spent over Greek roots don't arouse much enthusiasm, but let that last game be mentioned. We see the whole thing —just where the men stood on the bases, just how the ball was pitched, just how that famous hit saved the game! Have not we, who have cheered to victory or supported in defeat many a plucky team, a right to laud the athletic

glories of our Alma Mater? Athletics! They are the hope of our Republic. They develop the courage and vigor and fortitude which have made the Anglo-Saxon master of the world. The man who watches the contest catches its spirit, and goes away with a larger heart and a firmer will. Ever may the sons of Nassau Hall cultivate the generous and manly vigor of the true "foot-ball spirit."

In the fall there is a daily pilgrimage to the 'Varsity grounds to see the practice. Here are trained those foot-ball teams whose weights assume such enormous proportions in the college press. We have known a half-back to go up from one hundred and forty to one hundred and fifty-five pounds by the simple expedient of having his weight printed in *The Crimson* after a Harvard game. Here are developed those rushers who rush so hard that some of our friends can account for their prowess only on the hypothesis that they are drawing large salaries. The college lines-up along the ropes; every player is watched, and every good play enthusiastically cheered. Each spectator feels that the responsibility for the championship rests largely on his shoulders, and has his own views as to the wisdom of the captain's method of training. For two months nothing is heard but foot-ball. The papers are read only to see the scores of other teams, and former games are played over with a never-dying interest. The climax comes on Thanksgiving day, when we go to New York for the Yale game. The college goes *en masse*, leaving a score of musty bookworms and a dozen of stranded unfortunates in sole possession. Every man wears his orange-and-black button, and the Freshmen celebrate the first opportunity to wear colors by a prodigious display of orange ribbons on their umbrellas, canes, and hats.

Then the game! Thousands of people, gaily decorated coaches, a profusion of streamers, and a rattling fire of hostile cheers. A storm of applause announces the appearance of the teams. A little practice, and then the excitement rises to a pitch absolutely painful as the line-up is made and a dashing V opens the battle. How they play! We win, or else we don't. If we win, New York is n't large enough for us that night. Every man, woman, and child on Broadway seems to be wearing orange-and-black, the world was never so bright, the theatres are crowded with spectators more bent on celebrating than on seeing the play, and after midnight a tired and happy crowd boards the "owl" for Princeton, telling each other over and over again how it was done. If we lose, things are different.

The genus poller is never more distinct than during the foot-ball season. He rarely casts his shadow within the 'Varsity gates, and sometimes does not even know who are on the team. There is a tradition of a poller who was here for three years without knowing where the grounds were, but it does not appear to be well authenticated.

The base-ball returns with the robins, and with it the daily journey to the practice field is renewed. Princeton generally starts out with a championship team and rarely fails to win the first Yale game. Something often turns up before the end of the season and we don't get as many championships as we should, but while we are enjoying the prospect of victory everything is lovely. If it is our turn to go to New Haven, an eager crowd gathers in front of the telegraph office to hear returns an hour before there is a possibility of any news. A number of humorists take advantage of the opportunity to start false reports. One goes up-stairs to the office, then suddenly dashes down in wild excitement; his abettors at the door raise a cheer which is echoed over the whole campus. Princeton has won—seven to three! The Freshmen are delighted until they meet an upper classman, who smiles and says that the news never comes in so early. The waiting crowd relieves the suspense by singing and speculating.

At last the true word comes and we have won! No rest for the Freshmen that night! They must scour the town and country for a mile around in search of fuel. They determine that their fire shall be the biggest ever seen. Contracts are made for gallons of oil, and tar barrels sell at a premium. Prudent housekeepers have their front gates taken in and send their husbands out to watch the coops and dog-houses in the back yard. Gangs of suspicious-looking individuals in old clothes scout the streets and alleys, returning with a vast miscellany of boards, gates, panels of fence—anything that will burn. A few Juniors with the critical eye of professional builders direct the arrangement of the pile about the big cannon. Straw and tar barrels first, then boxes and rails; then everything that comes in. When the task is completed, the last can of oil poured on, and the dark pyramid, thirty or forty feet high, towers up in the centre of the quadrangle, the column is formed, and, with torches, horns, drums, banners, and fire-crackers, moves off in

ALBERT DOD HALL.

triumphal march. The President and some of the Faculty are visited and called upon for speeches. They come out on their piazzas and make a few remarks, in which every sentence is punctuated by a tremendous cheer. When the circuit is completed the celebrators return to the campus and apply the match. A column of flame shoots up through the tree-tops, and in the broad glare of the bonfire happy and contented groups stand about and discuss the full score just received. When the embers are burning to a dark red and the great clock in the belfry of Old North strikes midnight, the last stragglers retire to their rooms or go down to Dohm's to finish their discussion around a table.

Entrance examinations are scarcely over before a few zealous Juniors are busy getting the new class out for its first rush. With great care the word is circulated that the next night at ten the class will form back of the Observatory. The Sophomores are to be taken completely by surprise. The secret is so burdensome that the Freshmen gather in groups and talk earnestly under their breath in their efforts to keep it. They pass on the street with knowing looks, and exchange significant gestures. As a natural result, the Sophomores are generally in front of Reunion waiting for the fun to begin. What a delicious sense of conspiracy and adventure there is in that silent gathering for the first rush! Every approaching figure is scrutinized; rumor says the entire Sophomore class is lined-up back of Witherspoon. Scouts are sent out to work the dormitories and report on the enemy. And then, for the first time, the stillness is broken by three cheers for '9—! a challenge and defiance to the Sophomores. It is not a very good cheer; it is ragged and rough, and runs down at the end like an exhausted bag-pipe. But never mind, they mean it, and it is the old cheer. They will soon learn it better; they will ring it out with passionate enthusiasm in the critical moments of great games. It will proclaim the joy of many a victory, and when, after four years' cheering, with depleted ranks they stand for the last time on the steps of Old Nassau at the close of the last Senior singing, they will express their undying devotion to class and Alma Mater by a deep and sober chorus in that best of college cheers: "Rah! Rah! Rah! Tiger! Sis! Boom! Ah! Princeton!"

We have forgotten our Freshmen again; but the Juniors have been taking good care of them. By this time they are marching around

DICKINSON HALL.

the triangle singing "Here's to '9—," and working up courage for the impending conflict. At last the moment of destiny is come. They are lined up closely, eight abreast, the big men in front and the little men behind, ready to push for all they are worth. The column heads for the front campus gate, and a thrill of pleasure or fear runs down every spine as the sharp, clear-cut Sophomore cheer announces that the opposing forces are coming to dispute entrance. This is usually the signal for Mat. Goldie to step in and say : " Gentlemen, if there is a rush, every man in it will leave college to-morrow." Sometimes this is effective, but the blood of '9— is generally too warm to be cooled by the Proctor's eloquence. The Juniors pull their hats over their eyes and move among the Freshmen, suggesting that Mat. don't know them anyhow. A short parley, and then, with a fierce shout, at it they go. The two solid columns dash together — a violent collision, a few moments' desperate pushing in the densely packed masses, suddenly something gives way, and you are either joining in a rousing cheer for victory, or gathering the scattered forces for another charge. These rushes are comparatively harmless, and do a great deal to bring men together.

After the rush comes the pasting of the "procs," and then the cane-spree, and so one might go on indefinitely. But a complete narration of the whole medley of events which make up our varied existence would still fail to give its essence, the indefinable charm of that spirit which lingers about Nassau Hall and sheds its influence over all the petty incidents of college life. We feel it when, in those inextricable groups where every one seems to be reclining on every one else, we lie on the grass and listen to the Senior singing; it creeps over us when we stroll about the campus under the stars; it comes down with the moonbeams through the leaves of the whispering elms; and in after years, when the glad freedom of undergraduate life is past, and the whilom college boy has become a grave alumnus, and is pulling steadily in the traces on the dusty highway of life, betimes in day-dreams will come a fragrant breeze and the murmuring of elm leaves, and the eye of the grave alumnus will brighten. For, he says, it is a breath from the old campus, and in it whispers the spirit of Nassau Hall.

THE UNIVERSITY BOAT-HOUSE.

VIII.

THE PRINCETON IDEA.

In the eyes of many good people, Princeton stands for conservatism. It is doubtful whether most of them could tell just what this means, but on the whole there is a hazy idea that here things are not done just as the rest of the world does them. There is an impression that somewhere on the campus is the spot where Jonathan Edwards "stamped his iron heel," and that this sacred indentation is the fetich of every true son of Nassau Hall. To a Princeton man who really knows his Alma Mater and appreciates her spirit, all this is sufficiently amusing. To one who is in the strong, full current of undergraduate life, or who has felt the ardent and progressive spirit which dominates the Faculty in the work of the various departments, or in the more general concerns of college policy, the charge that Princeton is not in sympathy with modern progress can only provoke a smile.

And yet there is a sense in which Princeton

does not object to the charge of conservatism. The College of New Jersey is peculiarly fortunate in her traditions. She was founded and nurtured by men fired with the spirit which guided the two most important revolutions in the history of English-speaking peoples. The names of Princeton and Nassau Hall and the orange ribbon tell the story of her relation to the Revolution of 1688. Her five signatures to the Declaration of Independence, her twenty-nine members of the Continental Congress, and the historic room in Old North where that body held session, show her connection with the Revolution of 1776. The passionate love of liberty, hatred of pretence, manly independence and broad democratic spirit which characterized the men who founded Princeton and guided her early course have been cherished by succeeding generations. Princeton is proud of her past, and is not anxious to part from it. She finds in it the greatest inspiration for the present and the brightest promise for the future.

For Princeton is a college with a future. The atmosphere is full of it. Every one talks about the growth of the university, the development of the university spirit, the wonderful strides during the last twenty years and the anticipated advance of the next decade. The number of

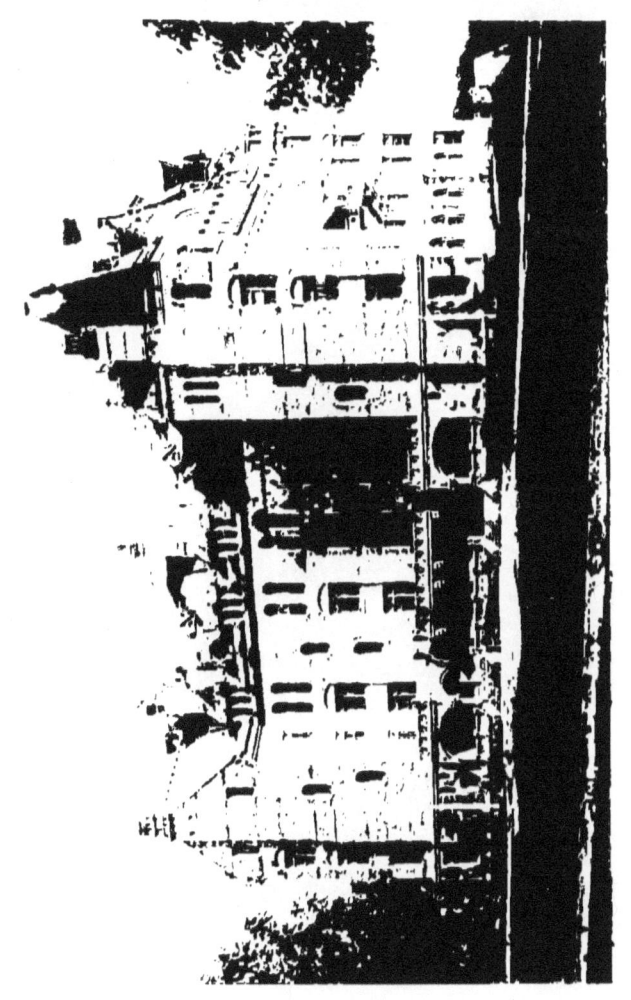

WITHERSPOON HALL.

students has about doubled in four years. The public college buildings, which have been completed or undertaken during the same period, equal the entire number in use when '91 were Freshmen. The Electrical and Chemical Schools have been added and furnished with splendidly equipped buildings. The Art School has been completed, and Dr. Prime has placed in it his magnificent collection. The Law School is talked of as a thing of the near future. Students and professors are caught by the enthusiasm of the movement. The latter are watching every opportunity to advance the college; the former organize sectional clubs to work up Princeton sentiment, and go out every summer a band of propagandists to campaign among their friends. All this is purely spontaneous. A normal Princeton man has an intense patriotism and an unalterable conviction that his friend makes the mistake of his life if he goes elsewhere. The result is that the size of recent Freshmen classes has been practically limited only by the accommodations. Dormitory rooms are at a premium, and the town is full of students. It seems that the buildings cannot be put up fast enough to relieve the pressure.

It is the combination of these two ideas which largely controls Princeton to-day—loyalty to the past and confidence in the future. They are not inharmonious; it is the connection between them which constitutes the conservatism of Nassau Hall. The future is not to be separated from the past, but built upon it; a structure growing so rapidly must have a broad foundation. The methods and policy which have stood the test of years are not to be thrown away for a theory. Progress must come by modification and development rather than by radical innovation. The gradual expansion of the curriculum and the evolution of the elective systems are illustrations. But what is of more concern here is the Princeton Idea as it affects undergraduate life. We all know the Harvard man and the Yale man; what are the influences which mould the Princeton man?

The first and most important is the social theory of the college. Here, most strikingly, one can observe the power and vitality of the traditional spirit. There is probably no other spot on the American continent quite so genuinely democratic as the Princeton campus. It is not that invidious distinctions are overlooked or kept under: they do not exist. The snob cannot survive in this atmosphere; he is either laughed out of his snobbishness or laughed out of college. The instincts of a gentleman, and a

THE CHEMICAL LABORATORY.

generous, manly spirit, are the only credentials. No lines are drawn, and every man fraternizes with his neighbor on the corner in front of Reunion. Here is the centre of our Republic. This space is to us what the Forum was to Rome. Is there some hitch in athletic matters? Has the Faculty become insubordinate, or is a college election approaching? Immediately there is a gathering of the clans and opinions are advanced, supported, and attacked with marvellous earnestness and force. For these congresses rain and snow have no terrors; umbrellas and storm-coats are brought into service, and the session continued. Men move from one group to another to hear the various oracles and advocate their own views. Before very long there is a substantial agreement, or else party lines are drawn and vigorously sustained until a mass-meeting in the English room settles the matter.

There is also an instinct for unity which manifests itself very strongly in the classes. The Freshmen are no sooner in college than the Seniors and Juniors begin to give them a great deal of good advice. "Try to get acquainted with every man in your class; don't wait for an introduction—introduce yourself as a classmate. Be very careful not to let your class get split up into factions." It might be thought that such a strong and self-conscious development of class feeling would break the college into four segments, but this is not the case. There is no axiom in Euclid more undisputed than this proposition: class spirit must yield to college spirit. The former is simply the regimental pride which does not affect the *esprit de corps* of the brigade. Not many colleges could do what Princeton did recently, when Junior captains maintained strict discipline over Seniors and Postgraduates on both of the 'Varsity teams. Yet here there was no difficulty whatever; the fitness of the men for their positions was recognized, and that was all-sufficient.

It must be confessed that Princeton is peculiarly fortunate in her opportunities for cultivating this broad college spirit. Here men are thrown together more than in any other institution of the size. Yale once had a meagre fence, which she prized as the Florentines did their Piazze. But even then we pitied her because she did not have a campus. What would Princeton do without her scrub athletics? Or if one is neither a ball-player nor a "lacrosse fiend," he can join one of the recumbent groups on the Front Campus, and smoke and chat and look up through the elms. Senior singing is

UNIVERSITY HALL.

preserved religiously. *The Princetonian* always urges the Seniors to come out, and the whole college gathers around the steps of Old North in the long summer twilight and listens to the familiar songs. This is a sacred rite—it means that Princeton men are one. The Senior chorus chants the hymn, and the listeners think of the time when they, too, will sit on those steps under the shadow of an approaching separation.

Princeton's two old halls have survived from the pre-Revolutionary period. Their records go back to a decade before the Declaration of Independence, and among the charter members they can point to such names as James Madison and William Paterson. All the American colleges at that early date had halls of a similar nature, but they have gradually disappeared before the rising tide of Greek-Letter Fraternities. The American Whig and Cliosophic societies have had many applications for charters from other institutions, but they have steadily refused to join the fraternity movement. This, too, may be called conservatism, but it is a conservatism which has given Princeton the best halls for oratory and debate in the country. Nearly every undergraduate is a member of one of them, and in each there is a select body of men who have come to Princeton largely on account of the opportunities which these halls offer, and who are training in parliamentary practice and public speaking under the influence of the venerable traditions of their chosen society. Nowhere else is the science of debate so carefully studied, or oratory more sedulously practised, and the annual contests on commencement stage arouse as much enthusiasm among the hallmen as a championship game in New York. Princeton's literary history is young, but the long roll of her sons who have become honored in the public service testifies to the wisdom of the policy which has preserved the old halls. Law students have told me that in their professional schools Princeton men are distinguished by the ease and readiness with which they address an audience, and the familiarity with which they use parliamentary forms. In their new and imposing marble buildings the societies have been true to their traditions. The club rooms are still subordinated to the library and the auditorium, and in their new homes we may expect Clio and Whig to train in the future, as in the past, men who will reflect honor alike on their college and their hall.

Here, too, the devotion to a broad college spirit is strikingly shown. These two great

REUNION HALL.

organizations fight vigorously enough for the supremacy, but their rivalry is confined to their own sphere. In athletics they are never heard of, and it is rare for them to enter class elections. The result is a freedom from those cliques and jealousies which so often mar the peace of fraternity colleges. When Princeton men hear of wrangles over athletic captains, or read of Senior classes giving up Class Day on account of fraternity feuds, they breathe a silent *Te Deum* for their own immunity. Fraternities were abolished in 1855, and now the undergraduates would not allow them to return. It is not because fraternities are objectionable in themselves, only they have no function here. In Cornell they aid the college materially by providing apartments for the men. In metropolitan colleges like Columbia they furnish a basis for social life; but here we have our college rooms, and prefer the broad, fraternal intercourse of dormitory and campus to the more limited friendship of the chapter-house. It is true we have our social clubs, with their clubhouses. In some respects they resemble the chapter-house, but only in a faint degree. The secrecy and the partisanship of the fraternity is wanting, and we may safely trust the genius of our institutions and the courtesy and public spirit of the club men to keep them from making any fracture in the unity of class or college.

In 1746 the President of His Majesty's Council granted a charter to the founders of the College of New Jersey " for that the said petitioners have also expressed their earnest desire that those of every religious denomination may have equal liberty and advantage of education, any different sentiments in religion notwithstanding"; and two years later the new Trustees expressed the hope to Governor Belcher that their infant college might "prove a flourishing seminary of piety and good literature." Princeton has been true to her traditions as a religious college. The curriculum has always preserved a place for Bible study; the philosophical chairs, while taking a liberal attitude towards the new evolutionary metaphysics, and recognizing its valuable contributions to the world's thought, have stood firmly on the fundamental principles of Christian theistic philosophy. Over half the members of the college are professing Christians, and the undergraduate life is dominated by Christian men. The Philadelphian Society was founded long before the college Y. M. C. A. came into existence, and fondly preserves the old name. It was in Princeton that the Students' Volunteer movement originated. Her

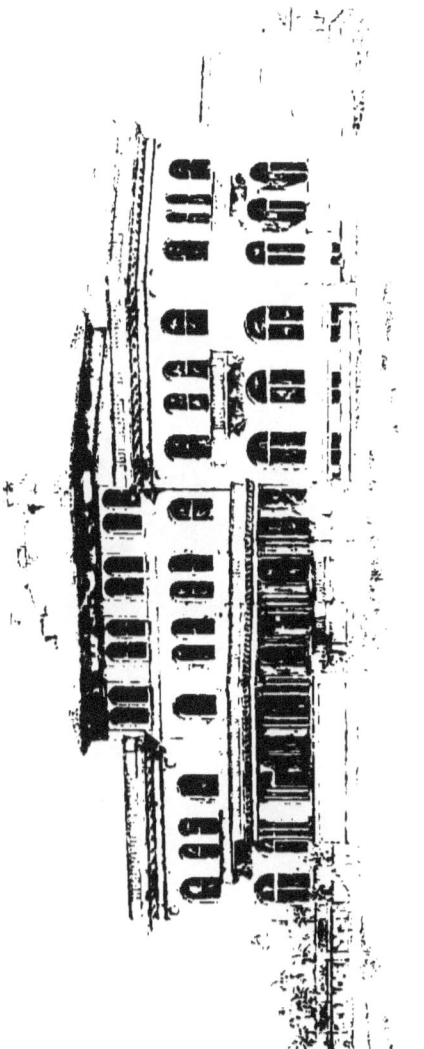

THE PRINCETON INN.

graduates have been most active in its expansion, and her undergraduates were the first to assume the support of a missionary in the foreign field.

While this is true, the spirit of the charter has been preserved in an utter absence of denominational feeling. The presence of the leading Presbyterian seminary in the same town has fostered a contrary belief, but nothing could be further from the truth. The first Board of Trustees under the charter was made up of Quakers, Episcopalians, and Presbyterians. Every Christian body is largely represented, and the Episcopalian students have a flourishing society of over a hundred members in connection with the parish church. In so large a collegiate body there are all kinds of men; but even the "sport," if he does not practise all the virtues, has at least an honest respect for them, which distinguishes him from most of his genus, and gives a brighter hope for his future.

If we were to attempt a picture of the ideal Princeton man, he would be first of all a gentleman; a man with a vigorous body, a true eye, a firm hand, and a sure foot. His spirit would be candid and prompt, his manner frank and genial, and over all would be shed the light of an exalted Christian character. This is the ideal. Sometimes a man comes near realizing it, but however far short the rest may come, the ideal is there, and some of its elements are bound to penetrate the character of every man who really breathes the spirit of Nassau Hall.

Monsieur de Coubertin, in his tour of the American colleges in 1889, heard some harsh criticisms on Princeton from men of a rival institution. He criticises her in some things himself, and justly; but on his second visit, with a remarkable insight, he catches and appreciates her true meaning. "I saw," he says, "that these were the true Americans, the backbone of the nation, the hope of the future; that in them repose traditions already venerable, the ancient sense, the moral vigor; that, finally, in them the present was closely linked to the past and perpetuated."

www.ingramcontent.com/pod-product-compliance
Lightning Source LLC
Chambersburg PA
CBHW031825230426
43669CB00009B/1229